Naima Abdul-Wahhab Abdullah

THE PATH TO JANNAH

Edited by:
Amel S. Abdullah

Cover by:
Hager El Nagdy

بسم الله الرحمن الرحيم

—In the name of Allah—

"THE REWARD OF DEEDS DEPENDS ON ONE'S INTENTIONS, AND EACH PERSON WILL BE REWARDED ACCORDING TO WHAT HE HAS INTENDED."

— A Saying of Prophet Muḥammad ﷺ (*Ṣaḥīḥ al-Bukhāri*, No. 6953)

A Word of Gratitude

"He who does not thank the people is not thankful to Allāh."

— A Saying of Prophet Muḥammad ﷺ (*Sunan Abī Dā'ūd,* No. 4811)

After first expressing my gratitude to the Almighty Creator Allāh ﷻ, Who provided me with the inspiration and capacity to write this book, I would also like to thank everyone who made it possible for this book to be published, including Sister Fatimaezzahra Lhabaz (the publisher of this work), my dear mother (who edited the English-language version), and Hager El Nagdy (who designed the cover).

I would also like to thank Anes Opardija and Benjamin Dogan for their assistance in translating this book into the German language.

I am also grateful to my father, my grandmother, and all of my loyal readers who enjoyed my previous books ("Islam Taught Me" and "Eternal Messages from the Quran") for the motivation they have provided me with to continue writing beneficial Islamic books. It is my hope that these works will inspire others to get closer to Allāh ﷻ and work with devotion to enter Jannah.

With that, I pray that Allāh ﷻ accepts this work and forgives me for any mistakes or shortcomings I was unaware of in my writings. May He gather all of us who are sincere in our love for Him in the Hereafter to be among the blessed inhabitants of Paradise. *Āmīn.*

— *Naima Abdullah*

Table of Contents

Introduction

"Praise be to Allāh, who has removed from us [all] sorrow."

— *Sūrat Fāṭir* (Qur'ān 35:34)

In all of our lives, we have undoubtedly experienced that blessed feeling of relief that usually follows a stressful event or situation. Whether the stress is fleeting or something more prolonged, the immense sense of relief that washes over a person's soul after hardship or calamity inevitably makes a believer turn toward the Creator in gratitude as one realizes the blessings that come with His guidance and protection.

If this is how we feel during our short time on Earth as we face various challenges, trials, temptations, and other struggles, imagine how these feelings multiply in the Hereafter if one has managed to pass the tests of this *dunyā* (worldly life).

This is reflected in the above-quoted verse of the Qur'ān, which shows that the inhabitants of Paradise will be overwhelmed with gratitude as they are admitted into their new abode and leave the sorrows of this world behind.

They, too, will experience a great sense of relief, but on a much bigger scale, because admission to Paradise is a rigorous and difficult process during which all of humanity is called to account for each and every thing we have done over the course of our lives, on a Day when nothing shall remain concealed.[1]

Yet no one will enter Paradise by his or her deeds alone, as it is only Allāh's forgiveness and mercy upon His faithful servants that grants one entry to His Eternal Gardens.[2]

1. Review Qur'ān 69:18.

2. As found in *Ṣaḥīḥ al-Bukhārī* (No. 6467).

When this trial ends by Allāh's will, then it is at this point that relief itself takes on new qualities, as the relief one feels in the Gardens of Paradise is unlike the relief of this *dunyā*. It is eternal, everlasting relief from all forms of sorrow, sadness, stress, or grief in a place where there is no mental or physical fatigue.[3] Feelings of loss, fear, disappointment, and even boredom do not exist there.

Called "Jannah" in Arabic, the Islamic concept of Paradise is nothing like the life of this world. It is a place free from imperfections, with special rewards for the believers who dwell there that "no eye has ever seen, no ear has ever heard of, and nobody has ever thought of," as conveyed to us by Prophet Muḥammad ﷺ, the last and final prophet of the heavenly revealed religions.[4]

Throughout history, people from different walks of life have attempted to portray the unique attributes of Paradise in paintings, films, and literature—yet all that we have seen (or imagined) in this worldly life is "nothing" compared to what Paradise actually is.[5]

As revealed by Allāh ﷻ in a verse from *Sūrat al-Sajdah*:

> "No soul knows what is kept hidden (in reserve) for them of joy (or delight) as a reward for what they used to do." (Qur'ān 32:17)

Names and Attributes of Paradise

Several names for Paradise are mentioned in the Qur'ān. Besides "Jannah," which means a garden with trees, we also find the following:

- Al-Dār al-Ākhirah (The Abode of the Hereafter) (Qur'ān 2:94);
- Dār al-Muttaqīn (The Abode of the Righteous) (Qur'ān 16:30);
- Dār al-Salām (The Abode of Peace) (Qur'ān 6:127);

3. Review Qur'ān 35:34–35.
4. As found in *Ṣaḥīḥ al-Bukhārī* (No. 4780).
5. Ibid.

- Jannāt ʿAdn (The Gardens of Eden or Perpetual Residence) (Qur'ān 9:72);
- Jannāt al-Naʿīm (The Gardens of Pleasure or Bliss) (Qur'ān 5:65);
- Jannāt al-Firdaws (The Gardens of Paradise, also described as the highest part of Paradise) (Qur'ān 18:107).

From these names alone, one can see that the Islamic concept of Paradise is that of an eternal dwelling place of extraordinary beauty and comfort that only hosts good people. It is peaceful, safe, and serene.

Although the reality of Jannah is far more magnificent than one can ever imagine, we find many other descriptions in the Qur'ān and authentic sayings of Prophet Muḥammad ﷺ that hint at what the righteous servants of Allāh ﷻ can expect to find there.

A Place of Great Bounties

The descriptions of Jannah from authentic sources tell us of a spacious garden as wide and vast as the heavens and earth having eight gates and different ranks of elevated status the higher one ascends, with the difference between every two ranks described as being like the difference between the heavens and the earth.[6]

The gardens are dark green in color, beneath which rivers are flowing.[7]

They are filled with the beauty of thornless lote trees[8] and an abundance of varied fruits that never go out of season and hang low on their branches so that they are always within reach. One will find clusters of bananas, grapes, dates, pomegranates, and any other fruit one desires. The fruits of Paradise are continuously replenished, just as the trees there provide perpetual shade, and these trees are stunning in appearance, with trunks made of gold.[9]

6. Review Qur'ān 3:133; 6:132. Also see *Jāmiʿ al-Tirmidhī* (No. 2531) and *Riyāḍ al-Ṣāliḥīn* (No. 1032).

7. Qur'ān 9:72; 55:64.

8. A unique tree that is only found in Jannah.

9. Qur'ān 13:35; 55:68; 56:20, 28–29, 32–33; 69:23; 78:32. Also see *Jāmiʿ al-Tirmidhī* (No. 2525).

As revealed in the Qur'ān, Allāh ﷻ describes some of the rivers found in Paradise as rivers of (fresh) water that always remains unaltered, rivers of milk whose taste never changes, rivers of purified honey, and rivers of delicious wine (that does not alter the mind).[10]

Familiar Yet Different

As stated by ʿAbd Allāh ibn al-ʿAbbās (RA): "Nothing in Paradise resembles anything in the life of this world except in name."[11]

This phenomenon is found described in the Qur'ān, such as when Allāh ﷻ tells us that the inhabitants of Jannah will feel surprised whenever they are provided with the exquisite fruits of Paradise, as these fruits will be similar to those they were familiar with in the worldly life of this *dunyā*, yet they will be different and much more delicious.[12]

Their dwelling places will be lofty, glass-like "chambers" (sometimes described in English translation as elevated mansions or palaces) that are safe, secure, and comfortable. Once the believers are in Paradise, they will recognize their new homes as though they have always been living there, the same way one recognizes his or her own home in this world.[13]

In Jannah, the weather is perfect; it is neither cold nor hot. In addition, one will never hear any idle talk there, including lies, backbiting, arguments, or vulgar speech; unlike the flawed life of this world, there will instead only be words of peace and harmony.[14]

Some of the other comforts enjoyed by the inhabitants of Jannah include garments made of silk and other luxuries[15] that only a few have experienced in the life of this world. In Jannah, however, these comforts belong to all of its inhabitants and are also far superior to anything found in this *dunyā*.

10. Qur'ān 37:47; 47:15.

11. *al-Jāmiʿ al-Ṣaghīr* (No. 7614).

12. Qur'ān 2:25.

13. Qur'ān 34:37; 39:20; 47:6. Also see *Jāmiʿ al-Tirmidhī* (No. 1984).

14. Qur'ān 56:25–26; 76:13.

15. Review Qur'ān 18:31 among other verses.

Memories and Flashbacks

Overwhelmed by all of the joy and blessings they are surrounded with as they are reunited with the righteous among their loved ones and granted the privilege of seeing all of the prophets as well as our exalted Lord and Creator Allāh ﷻ, the inhabitants of Jannah will start wondering what led them to attain the bounties of Paradise—and several "flashbacks" of how they spent their short time on Earth will come to mind as they recall key points that can, *in shā' Allāh*, help guide those of us who still live within the confines of this *dunyā*.[16]

Among other things, the people of Jannah will remember that what kept them on the path of righteousness in this life was their unwavering faith in Allāh's promises to them as revealed in the Glorious Qur'ān—and they will find themselves saying with a complete sense of satisfaction and gratitude:

> "Praise be to Allāh, who has fulfilled for us His promise and made us inherit the earth [so] we may settle in Paradise [Jannah] wherever we will. And excellent is the reward of [righteous] workers." (Qur'ān 39:74)

A Road-map to Jannah and A Special Prayer

In the following pages, my dear readers, we will take a closer look at what the inhabitants of Paradise actually remember about their deeds in this worldly life, with the hope that this information may serve as a road-map for those of us who are striving for Allāh's pleasure in order to attain Jannah for ourselves and our loved ones. In order to do that by Allāh's will, we need to cultivate the traits of a believer along with a solid understanding of our true mission in the temporary life of this world so that we can take concrete steps toward achieving this important goal.

16. Qur'ān 4:69; 13:23; 52:25–26; 75:23.

To highlight the importance of these traits, each chapter of this book starts with a relevant *ḥadīth* or verse from the Qur'ān, while the keys traits associated with these verses and quotes are listed in the Table of Contents for easier navigation of the various topics.

Before I leave you now to take what I pray will be a beneficial and enriching journey on the path to Jannah, *in shā' Allāh*, I will end with a short prayer (*du'ā'*) recited by Prophet Ibrāhīm (Abraham) (PBUH) that we, too, should all make it a habit to recite:

"O my Lord! Bestow wisdom on me, and join me with the righteous, and grant me a mention [i.e., reputation] of honor among later generations, and make me among the inheritors of Jannāt al-Na'īm [the Gardens of Bliss]."[17] *Āmīn*.

17. Qur'ān 26:83–85.

They have taqwá (piety)

"The best provision is *taqwá* [piety]."

— *Sūrat al-Baqarah* (Qur'ān 2:197)

At some point during their worldly lives, the inhabitants of Jannah discovered an important secret: **The life of this *dunyā* is nothing but a short trip that everyone must take before reaching the final destination of eternity...**

And just as we would ordinarily prepare for a trip by making a list of necessary supplies we should bring with us in order for the journey to be one that is both successful and pleasant, the people of Jannah knew that they would need a **huge supply of *taqwá*** in order for them to survive the journey of life and pass all of the tests along the way.

As such, this understanding was reflected in all aspects of their worldly lives, including their speech, their everyday deeds, and their relationships with others.

Often translated to English as **piety, righteousness, or fear of Allāh**, the Arabic word *taqwá* is originally derived from a word that means **protective barrier or shield**, as it creates a protective shield that prevents one from committing sinful acts that are displeasing to Allāh ﷻ.

Those who do not fortify themselves with *taqwá* in this worldly life are in danger of failing the tests of this *dunyā*, as Allāh ﷻ provides us with ample opportunity to cultivate this important trait throughout our lives. In fact, He is continuously offering us guidance through His signs even in times of hardship and temptation, and people who deliberately choose to reject this guidance (and thus lack *taqwá*) will find themselves unequipped to pass such tests.

Deliberate rejection of Allāh's guidance is also something that leads to arrogance, which in turn gives rise to corruption, oppression, and other forms of injustice.

Firʿawn, the oppressive pharaoh of his time, is a prime example of this.[18] Despite the many opportunities he was granted in different situations over a period of many years to repent to Allāh ﷻ, he persisted in corruption and tyranny as he continuously challenged Prophet Mūsá (Moses) (PBUH) and the believers from Banī Isrāʾīl (the Israelites) without shame, remorse, or *taqwá* (fear of Allāh ﷻ).

Each time he and his wicked companions were tested with hardship, however, they would tell Mūsá (PBUH): "O Mūsá, invoke for us your Lord by what He has promised you. If you [can] remove the punishment from us, we will surely believe you."[19]

But each time Allāh ﷻ removed the hardship in response to these pleas, they would soon return to their evil ways![20]

This pattern of ungrateful arrogance continued until one day it was too late for Firʿawn as he drowned in the sea and declared himself a believer, saying: "I believe that there is no deity except that in whom the Israelites believe, and I am of the Muslims."[21]

Allāh ﷻ did not accept this declaration, instead reminding Firʿawn that he had always been keen to disobey and was of the corrupters.[22]

This is the state of the disbelievers in general, who do not take advantage of their time on Earth to do good deeds. Allāh ﷻ tells us: "When death comes to one of them, he says, 'My Lord, send me back so that I may do righteousness in that which I neglected.'"[23] But by then, it is too late.

To avoid such a fate, follow the advice of Prophet Muḥammad ﷺ, who said: "Have *taqwá* wherever you are."[24]

---

18. Allāh ﷻ tells us his story in several chapters of the Qurʾān (for example, see Qurʾān 7:103–137).
19. Qurʾān 7:134.
20. Qurʾān 7:135.
21. Qurʾān 10:90.
22. Qurʾān 10:91.
23. Qurʾān 23:99–100.
24. *Riyāḍ al-Ṣāliḥīn* (No. 61).

The inhabitants of Jannah will remember having *taqwá* in this worldly life, as evidenced by them telling one other: **"Indeed, we were previously among our people fearful [of displeasing Allāh], so Allāh conferred favor upon us and protected us from the punishment of the Scorching Fire."**[25]

It is no coincidence that Allāh ﷻ describes Jannah as a place exclusively "prepared for the people of *taqwá*."[26] He also tells us that He loves the people of *taqwá*[27] and will "make a way out" for them (providing relief from distress), also providing for them from (sources) they cannot imagine.[28]

But before we learn more about the characteristics of those whom Allāh ﷻ has favored over all people on Earth[29] (and I pray we are among them, *in shā' Allāh*), let us first take a deeper look at the concept of faith itself, as without faith there will be no *taqwá*, and thus no Jannah as a reward.

25. Qur'ān 52:26–27.
26. Qur'ān 3:133.
27. Qur'ān 3:76.
28. Qur'ān 65:2–3.
29. See Qur'ān 49:13 and *Musnad Aḥmad* (No. 23489).

They are believers

"And upon their Lord they rely."

— *Sūrat al-Anfāl* (Qur'ān 8:2)

Faith starts with one's belief in the existence of God (Allāh).

But what does it mean to believe in His existence?

Above all else, it means to believe that Allāh ﷻ is the One and Only Creator, and that He alone is worthy of worship.[30] A Muslim believes that there is **no similarity** whatsoever between the Creator and anyone or anything created by Him,[31] which in turn means that we do not sanctify any of His prophets, angels, or other creations.[32]

An understanding of Allāh's varied names and attributes shows us that He is:

- al-Malik (The King, The Sovereign) (Qur'ān 20:114);
- al-ʿAlīm (The All-Knowing, The Omniscient) (Qur'ān 6:101);
- al-ʿAzīz (The Exalted in Might) (Qur'ān 59:23);
- al-Jabbār (The All-Powerful, The Omnipotent) (Qur'ān 59:23);
- al-Razzāq (The Ever-Providing) (Qur'ān 51:58);
- al-Wahhāb (The Supreme Bestower) (Qur'ān 3:8);
- al-Karīm (The Bountiful, The Generous) (Qur'ān 27:88);
- al-Mujīb (The Responsive, the Answerer) (Qur'ān 11:61);
- al-Wadūd (The Loving, The Kind) (Qur'ān 11:90);
- al-Wakīl (The Trustee, The Dependable) (Qur'ān 11:12);
- al-Walī (The Protecting Friend, Patron, and Helper) (Qur'ān 4:45).[33]

30. Review Qur'ān 2:163.

31. Review Qur'ān 42:11.

32. Review Qur'ān 3:79–80.

33. These are just a few of Allāh's many names that a believer may wish to use when calling out to the Creator during supplications and prayers.

As such, belief in Allāh ﷻ means that we ask Him alone for help with life's problems, without any intermediaries, as it is He alone who can remove our afflictions and provide for us when we are in need.

The inhabitants of Jannah will remember their trust and faith in the Creator as they tell one another: "**Indeed, we used to call upon [i.e., worship] Him before. Indeed, it is He who is the Beneficent, the Merciful.**"[34]

Faith in Allāh ﷻ also means that a person must believe in resurrection after death and the existence of the Hereafter.

Regarding this, Allāh ﷻ tells us in the Qur'ān that one of the inhabitants of Jannah will remember that he once had a companion on Earth who used to say to him in dissuasion: "Are you indeed of those who believe that when we have died and become dust and bones, we will indeed be recompensed?"

Then he will look to see what became of that companion and find him in the midst of Hell-Fire.

With the knowledge that his faith had saved him, the believer will tell his old companion: "By Allāh, you almost ruined me. If not for the favor of my Lord, I would have been of those brought in [to Hell]."

Then he will say: "Indeed, this [i.e., the place where I am now] is the great attainment."[35]

This is one of the many lessons and reminders from the people of Jannah to remain steadfast in faith, as we are all vulnerable to encountering a bad companion who attempts to divert us away from the path to Jannah, whether that person is someone close to us, an influential acquaintance, or someone we listen to or follow online. Sometimes we may also be led astray by the books we read or even by misguided inner thoughts that eventually lead to one's own destruction.

---

34. Qur'ān 52:28.

35. For the whole story, review Qur'ān 37:51–60.

Do not let such trials defeat you, as one must continuously strive for Jannah despite the challenges we find along the way.

There are many other facets to belief in Allāh ﷻ, including the belief that Allāh ﷻ has sent prophets and messengers to guide humanity at different times. As Muslims, we believe that Muḥammad ﷺ is the last and final prophet, and that the Qur'ān is the only remaining authentic revelation from God (Allāh) that has not been changed or distorted.

Believers have certain other traits in common, as found in this verse from *Sūrat al-Anfāl*:

"The believers are only those who, when Allāh is mentioned, their hearts become fearful, and when His verses are recited to them, it increases them in faith; and upon their Lord they rely."[36]

36. Qur'ān 8:2.

They Give Charity and Maintain Their Prayers

"And whoever believes in Allāh - He will guide his heart."

— *Sūrat al-Taghābun* (Qur'ān 64:11)

As the inhabitants of Jannah converse with each other and recall how they passed the tests of this worldly life in order to attain the eternal blessings of their final abode in Paradise, they will also start wondering about those who transgressed and found themselves in Hell-Fire.

In a dialogue with the wrong-doers that takes place with a barrier between them, they will ask them: "What put you into Saqar?"[37]

In response, the people of Hell-Fire will say: "We were not of those who prayed."[38]

What is the connection between faith, prayer, and one's final abode?

The answer is in this verse from *Sūrat al-'Ankabūt*: "**Indeed, prayer prohibits immorality and wrongdoing.**"[39]

Some may wonder why it is not sufficient for one to have faith in the heart. Can't someone still be a decent human being without committing to prayers?

It is easy to assume so theoretically, but praying whenever one wishes (or not praying at all) means that one has severed an important connection with Allāh ﷻ and forgotten his or her main purpose in life, which in turn hardens the heart and produces feelings of negativity, despair, and worthlessness.

Allāh ﷻ, Who is the most knowing of this fact, tells us:

"Indeed, mankind was created anxious: When evil touches him, [he is] impatient, and when good touches him, [he is] withholding [of it], **except**

37. Qur'ān 74:42. Saqar is one of the names of Hell and means a place of burning.

38. Qur'ān 74:43.

39. Qur'ān 29:45.

the observers of prayer – those who are steadfast in their prayers."[40]

It follows that **maintaining the five obligatory prayers required of a Muslim is deeply linked to one's belief in Allāh ﷻ, and the two cannot be separated from one another.**

Another thing the people of Hell-Fire will regret not doing while they still had the chance in the worldly life of this *dunyā* is not feeding the poor although they had the ability to do so.[41]

It is no coincidence that those who are stingy with Allāh ﷻ (by not praying or allocating time for worship) are also stingy with people (by not providing for their most basic of needs).

Allāh ﷻ says: "And let not those who [greedily] withhold what Allāh has given them of His bounty ever think that it is better for them. Rather, it is worse for them. Their necks will be encircled by what they withheld on the Day of Resurrection."[42]

Someone who takes sincere steps to know the Creator and also believes in Him and maintains his or her relationship with Him through prayer cannot be other than a generous, kind, soft-hearted person; this is why Prophet Muḥammad ﷺ said that **no one "truly believes until he loves for his brother what he loves for himself."**[43]

Based on above, it is easy to understand why Allāh ﷻ tells us:

"The ones who establish prayer, and from what We have provided them, they spend, **those are the believers, truly.** For them are degrees [of high position] with their Lord and forgiveness and noble provision."[44]

40. Qur'ān 70:19–23.

41. Review Qur'ān 74:44.

42. Qur'ān 3:180.

43. *Riyāḍ al-Ṣāliḥīn* (No. 183).

44. Qur'ān 8:3–4.

All of this shows why **faith is the foundation the inhabitants of Jannah will have built upon to further cultivate their other positive qualities**, the most important of which is *taqwá,* which leaves one's heart open and receptive to guidance and results in improved character and values in this worldly life—ultimately allowing one to attain the pleasure of our Lord, Allāh ﷻ, Who says:

"Whoever does righteousness, whether male or female, **while he is a believer**- We will surely cause him to live a good life, and We will surely give them their reward [in the Hereafter] according to the best of what they used to do."[45]

Let us now explore together some of the other praiseworthy traits that the people of Jannah will have acquired due to their faith and *taqwá*.

45. Qur'ān 16:97.

They control their tongues

"And they had been guided [in worldly life] to good speech."

— *Sūrat al-Ḥajj* (Qur'ān 22:24)

Good speech is positivity, kindness, and mercy towards others.

It is to be truthful, and to refrain from backbiting and idle talk.

It also means controlling one's tongue when not in a good mood and responding to the bad moods of others with wisdom, either through silence or the ability to say something uplifting or beneficial that may actually help the situation.

Prophet Muḥammad ﷺ has informed us that "**the faith of a worshiper is not upright until his heart is upright, and his heart is not upright until his tongue is upright.**"[46]

To maintain the uprightness of their tongues that would not utter bad language even during times of calamity or hardship, the inhabitants of Jannah will have benefited from the great variety of expressions Islām has taught us to use in difficult circumstances.

Before looking at some examples below, let us keep in mind that **the deliberate use of good words instead of bad ones reflects faith, trust, respect, *taqwá*, and shyness from Allāh** ﷻ, because a believer knows that Allāh ﷻ is aware of our hardships and does not ever abandon His righteous servants.

During times of helplessness, fear, or oppression, one can say:

Ḥasbunā Allāhu wa ni'ma al-Wakīl

"Allāh is sufficient for us, and He is the best Disposer of affairs."

46. *Musnad Aḥmad* (No. 13047).

A story associated with this phrase took place after the early Muslims had been defeated by the non-believers in the Battle of Uḥud and learned that the non-believers had prepared a great army to further attack the Muslims in Madīnah, where they lived.

One can imagine the great difficulty of this situation. Not only had the Muslims just lost a large number of their beloved family members and companions, but those who survived were also undoubtedly exhausted due to wounds and injuries suffered during the battle—yet they did not run away or give up and instead faced the situation bravely, because they knew that Allāh ﷻ was by their side.

In a passage from *Sūrat Āli ʿImrān*, we find that the hypocrites tried to instill fear in the Muslims by telling them that their enemies had mobilized forces against them, but "it [merely] increased them in faith, and they said: **Sufficient for us is Allāh, and [He is] the best Disposer of affairs.**" After this, "they returned with favor from Allāh and bounty, [with] no harm having touched them, for they sought to please Allāh."[47]

During times of loss and calamity, one can say:

Innā li-llāhi wa-innā ilayhi rājiʿūn

"To Allāh we belong, and to Allāh we return."

Allāh ﷻ promises that His blessings will be upon those who are patient and bound fast their hearts with this phrase, as they are indeed the guided ones.[48]

We can also learn from the example of Prophet Muḥammad ﷺ, who displayed great sadness when his son Ibrāhīm died at a young age, yet was still mindful of pleasing Allāh ﷻ in his sorrow and said as he wept:

"The eyes are shedding tears and the heart is grieved, and we will not say except what pleases our Lord. And indeed, O Ibrāhīm, we are grieved by your departure."[49]

47. Qur'ān 3:173–174.
48. Review Qur'ān 2:156–157.
49. *Riyāḍ al-Ṣāliḥīn* (No. 927).

Other phrases we are encouraged to use in different circumstances include:

Subḥān Allāh

"Glory be to Allāh."

Al-ḥamdu lillāh

"Praise be to Allāh."

Lā ilāha illa Allāh

"There is no deity but Allāh."

Allāhu Akbar

"Allāh is the Greatest."

Because of the great blessings they hold, the Prophet ﷺ said that the uttering of these words was dearer to him than everything else in the world.[50] He also said that saying *lā ḥawla wa lā quwwatah illā billāh* ("There is no strength or power except with Allāh") grants a person one of the treasures of Jannah.[51]

There are many other examples from the *sīrah* (biography) of Prophet Muḥammad ﷺ that show how the Prophet ﷺ always maintained the Islamic etiquette of good speech.

One such example involves Anas ibn Mālik (RA), who worked as a servant in the Prophet's household for a period of time and described his experience there, saying: "I served Allāh's Messenger ﷺ for ten years, and he never said 'Uff!'[52] to me. He never asked me about something I had done, saying, 'Why did you do that?' Nor [did he ever ask me] about something I had left undone, saying, 'Why did you leave it undone?'"[53]

The Prophet ﷺ also informed us that the etiquettes associated with good speech guarantee one a house in Jannah:

---

50. *Riyāḍ al-Ṣāliḥīn* (No. 1409).
51. *Ṣaḥīḥ al-Bukhārī* (No. 6384).
52. An expression of displeasure.
53. *al-Shamā'il al-Muḥammadiyyah* (No. 344).

"I guarantee a house in the surroundings of Paradise (Jannah) for a man who avoids quarrelling even when he is in the right, a house in the middle of Paradise for a man who avoids lying even when he is joking, and a house in the upper part of Paradise for a man who makes his character good."[54]

54. *Sunan Abī Dā'ūd* (No. 4800).

THEY ARE PATIENT WITH THE TRIALS OF THIS LIFE

"Peace be upon you for what you patiently endured."

— *Sūrat al-Ra'd* (Qur'ān 13:24)

The road to Jannah is not paved with roses; there are many difficult tests and trials in the worldly life of this *dunyā* that may cause a person of weak faith to lose sight of the ultimate goal of Jannah that we are all striving for as Muslims.

This may especially be the case if one is surrounded by a large number of temptations or people who do not live according to the same moral code found in Islām. Such people may even make you feel that you are extreme for following the most basic of Islamic teachings, such as praying, fasting, or wearing the *ḥijāb*.

This is why Prophet Muḥammad ﷺ said: "Hell-Fire is draped with all kinds of desires and passions, while Jannah is draped with adversities."[55]

And this is also why the angels will greet the believers at the gates of Jannah by saying: "**Peace be upon you for what you patiently endured. And excellent is the final abode.**"[56]

The inhabitants of Jannah will have exercised a high level of patience in this *dunyā*, causing them to shun worldly temptations and recognize life's other challenges as opportunities to pass the tests we are all presented with on a daily basis, such as illness and other calamities. When dealing with difficult people (and circumstances), those destined for Jannah restrain their anger and do not seek misplaced revenge.

Allāh ﷻ tells us that someone who exercises this level of patience and self-restraint is among the fortunate.[57]

55. *Riyāḍ al-Ṣāliḥīn* (No. 101).

56. Qur'ān 13:24.

57. See Qur'ān 41:34–35.

A man once insulted Abū Bakr al-Ṣiddīq (RA), who was Prophet Muḥammad's closest friend and companion. Abū Bakr (RA) initially remained silent, but then answered him back when the man went too far. The Prophet ﷺ showed displeasure at what Abū Bakr (RA) had done and left. Abū Bakr (RA) then followed him and asked the Prophet ﷺ why he was displeased. The Prophet ﷺ responded that an angel had been supporting him and answering for him the whole time he was silent, but when he answered for himself, the angel left and Satan came instead, and the Prophet ﷺ could not sit in the same place where Satan was.[58]

The patience exercised by the inhabitants of Jannah will have extended to every aspect of their worldly lives, also preventing them from illicit relationships outside of marriage,[59] which means they will have maintained respectful boundaries with the opposite gender and also lowered their gazes, whether in "real" life or on social media.

Prophet Muḥammad ﷺ tells us that among the seven types of people whom Allāh ﷻ will give from His shade, on a Day when there is no shade except for His [The day of Resurrection], is "a man whom an extremely beautiful woman seduces (for illicit relations), but he (rejects this offer and) says: 'I fear Allāh.'"[60]

As alluded to above, patience also means having a positive attitude when adversity strikes, and to remain steadfast when performing Islamic rituals such as praying and fasting.

58. *Sunan Abī Dā'ūd* (No. 4896).

59. Refer to Qur'ān 70:29–31.

60. *Riyāḍ al-Ṣāliḥīn* (No. 449).

They seek forgiveness for their sins

"And [they] sought forgiveness for their sins."

— *Sūrat Āli 'Imrān* (Qur'ān 3:135)

Certain people will obtain the rewards of Jannah despite their sins and shortcomings. This is because they are humble and do not persist in sin when they have wronged themselves or others during moments of human weakness. Instead, their hearts fill with regret as they remember Allāh ﷻ. They immediately seek forgiveness, correct any harms that have been done, and refrain from committing the same mistakes.

Yet some people find it difficult to stop sinning no matter how hard they try.

Once upon a time, there was a man who used to commit all kinds of sins. He used to drink alcohol, steal, gamble, and even murder people. Although he wished to reform himself, he never succeeded. So, finally he went to a wise man and asked him for advice. The wise man told him: "Just promise me to stop one sin you are committing, which is lying."

The man was surprised. "Lying? This is the least serious sin I commit."

The wise man said, "So, do you promise me not to lie for the rest of your life?"

"I promise," said the man.

Days passed, and the man wanted to drink alcohol, but then he thought about the promise he had made. "What will I say if the wise man asks me if I am still drinking? I don't want him to think badly of me. Maybe I should just throw the bottle away so that I don't have to lie." After that, each time the man wanted to commit a sin, he could not bring himself to do it because of his promise to stay truthful.

While the above is just a story and not something that is recorded in the books of *ḥadīth* or Islamic history, it illustrates an important point, as the Prophet ﷺ emphasized the importance of truthfulness when he said: "You must be **truthful. Truthfulness leads to dutifulness, and dutifulness leads to Jannah.** A man continues to tell the truth he until he is recorded as a truthful man with Allāh. Beware of lying. **Lying leads to deviance, and deviance leads to Hell-Fire.** A man continues to lie until he is recorded as a liar with Allāh."[61]

Fasting is another important strategy for quelling harmful or destructive desires. In Arabic, fasting is known as *ṣiyām*, the literal meaning of which is to abstain.

While the Islamic fast requires one to abstain from food and drink from dawn until dusk, those who understand the many wisdoms behind fasting also recognize the treasures contained in the following verse of the Qur'ān: "O you who believe, fasting is prescribed for you as it was prescribed for those before you **that you may become righteous.**"[62]

It is not befitting of a fasting person to use bad language or engage in sinful behavior, and this is why the true spirit of fasting requires one to abstain from sinful behaviors in general.[63] In addition, fasting requires that one be truthful with Allāh ﷻ; otherwise, one has not truly fasted.

Those who adhere to the true spirit of fasting with sincere intentions will enter Jannah through a special gate called al-Rayyān, which is exclusively for those who fast and not open to anyone else.[64]

In the end, it is not sins themselves that lead to punishment in the Hereafter, but rather being too proud to repent from them along with the forgetfulness of Allāh ﷻ, both of which ultimately lead to failing the tests of this *dunyā*.

"Indeed, Allāh loves those who always turn to Him in repentance, and He loves those who purify themselves."[65]

---

61. *al-Adab al-Mufrad* (No. 386).
62. Qur'ān 2:183.
63. Based on a saying of the Prophet ﷺ (see *Sunan Ibn Mājah*, No. 1689).
64. See *Sunan al-Nasā'ī* (No. 2237).
65. Qur'ān 2:222.

THEY KEEP THEIR PROMISES

"And those who are to their trusts and promises attentive."

— *Sūrat al-Ma'ārij* (Qur'ān 70:32)

Islām gives great importance to being just with others and keeping promises. Some examples of this from the Qur'ān are found in the following verses:

- "Allāh orders justice and good conduct and giving [help] to relatives and forbids immorality and bad conduct and oppression." (Qur'ān 16:90)
- "...And do not break oaths after their confirmation while you have made Allāh, over you, a security [i.e., witness]." (Qur'ān 16:91)
- "Indeed, Allāh commands you to render trusts to whom they are due and when you judge between people to judge with justice." (Qur'ān 4:58)
- "And do not take your oaths as [means of] deceit between you, lest a foot slip after it was [once] firm, and you would taste evil [in this world] for what [people] you diverted from the way of Allāh,[66] and you would have [in the Hereafter] a great punishment." (Qur'ān 16:94)

It is required of a believing Muslim to fully understand and apply these concepts by always striving to keep his or her promises and being truthful in all of his or her dealings with others, which encompasses many facets of life, such as marriage, financial agreements, and other types of contracts (to name just a few).

Those who are granted entry to Paradise in the Hereafter will have also demonstrated an understanding of the following words of the Prophet ﷺ, who told us:

"All of you are guardians and are responsible for your subjects."[67]

66. This is in reference to non-Muslims who are left with a bad impression about Islām due to their interactions with Muslims who are dishonest or do not conduct their lives according to Islamic values.

67. See *Riyāḍ al-Ṣāliḥīn* (No. 283).

Regardless of one's social status in the temporary world of this *dunyā*, such people will have lived their lives with a great sense of responsibility, going above and beyond ordinary requirements in order to achieve excellence in all of their worldly responsibilities. As such, the inhabitants of Jannah will undoubtedly include a wide variety of people from diverse backgrounds, such as teachers who behaved as proper role models for their students in this life, writers who presented the truth of Islām in their writings, healthcare providers who worked in devotion to their patients and kept their affairs confidential, parents who worked hard to provide for their families, children who helped their parents and served as role models for their younger siblings...

In addition to the above, modern-day life has presented new challenges that one must be aware of in order to attain success in the Hereafter. Those who are active on social media, for example, must understand that they are responsible for what they share with their followers, including any images that may be prohibited for a believer to look at.

One must also weigh his or her words carefully in order to avoid vain discourse, which is something that may cause those who engage in it to be punished by Allāh ﷻ,[68] as this type of pointless talk is something that results in wasted time and frequently creates bitterness and animosity among a large number of people when one could instead be using such platforms to spread goodness and beneficial ideas to motivate others and stimulate intellect among those who are reading.

68. See Qur'ān 74:45.

Do you ever feel that you are just aimlessly doing things without thinking about the guardianship that the Prophet ﷺ spoke about?

No matter what we are occupied with, we should all periodically ask ourselves whether we are truly taking responsibility for the things we do in life and how these things may impact others.

Allāh ﷻ tells us that in the Hereafter, those condemned to the fires of Hell will call out begging to the inhabitants of Jannah: "Pour upon us some water or from whatever Allāh has provided you (for your sustenance)!"[69]

But the inhabitants of Jannah will tell them that Allāh ﷻ has forbidden these things to those who disbelieved in Allāh ﷻ and took their religion as distraction and amusement and were deluded by the life of this world.[70]

About this, Allāh ﷻ says: "So, today We will forget them just as they forgot the meeting of this Day of theirs and for having rejected Our verses."[71]

Rejecting Allāh's verses is not just about the clear *kufr* (disbelief) that comes with the rejection of Allāh ﷻ. It could also mean abandoning the Qur'ān and not implementing what it says.

"O Allāh, help me to remember You, to give You thanks, and to perform Your worship in the best manner."[72] *Āmīn*.

69. See Qur'ān 7:50.

70. See Qur'ān 7:50–51.

71. Qur'ān 7:51.

72. A supplication made by Prophet Muḥammad ﷺ (see *Ḥiṣn al-Muslim*, No. 59).

THEY HUMBLY SUBMIT TO ALLĀH ﷻ

"We hear and we obey. [We seek] Your forgiveness, our Lord, and to You is the [final] destination."

— *Sūrat al-Baqarah* (Qur'ān 2:285)

Allāh ﷻ says: "O you who have believed, enter into Islām completely [and perfectly] and do not follow the footsteps of Satan. Indeed, he is to you a clear enemy."[73]

The above means that a believer must fully submit to the commands of Allāh ﷻ rather than picking and choosing what he or she finds convenient while ignoring the rest for the sake of pleasing others or adhering to cultural traditions or personal desires that conflict with the teachings of Islām.

For example, one might claim to be a believer, yet not put any effort into worshiping Allāh ﷻ. On the other hand, there are those who regularly perform Islamic rituals, such as praying or fasting, but do not implement important values, such as maintaining family ties, giving charity, or being kind to others. Still others seem to "forget" (or ignore) Islamic guidelines for respectful interaction between the two genders in various circumstances, whether it is online, in the workplace, or at an event like a wedding.

Allāh ﷻ tells us that we should "seek refuge in Allāh" whenever Satan comes to us with such temptations or evil suggestions.[74] He also tells us who the companions of the righteous will be in Paradise by His will:

"And whoever obeys Allāh and the Messenger - those will be with the ones upon whom Allāh has bestowed favor of the prophets, the steadfast affirmers of truth, the martyrs and the righteous. And excellent are those as companions."[75]

73. Qur'ān 2:208.
74. Qur'ān 41:36.
75. Qur'ān 4:69.

This shows that a believer must put effort into pleasing Allāh ﷻ in order to attain the honor of being among the companions of the prophets and Allāh's other righteous servants in Jannah. One can achieve this by consistently obeying the teachings of Allāh ﷻ and His Messenger ﷺ, which means submitting to the Creator and asking for His help to do so.

Special supplications for this purpose include the entirety of *Sūrat al-Fātiḥah* (which we already recite on a daily basis in all of our prayers) and the last two verses of *Sūrat al-Baqarah*:

- "In the name of Allāh, Most Gracious, Most Merciful. [All] praise is [due] to Allāh, Lord of the worlds - The Entirely Merciful, the Especially Merciful, Sovereign of the Day of Recompense. It is You we worship and You we ask for help. Guide us to the straight path, the path of those upon whom You have bestowed favor, not of those who have earned [Your] anger or of those who are astray." (Qur'ān 1:1–7)
- "We hear and we obey. [We seek] Your forgiveness, our Lord, and to You is the [final] destination. Our Lord, do not impose blame upon us if we have forgotten or erred. Our Lord, and lay not upon us a burden like that which You laid upon those before us. Our Lord, and burden us not with that which we have no ability to bear. And pardon us; and forgive us; and have mercy upon us. You are our protector, so give us victory over the disbelieving people." (Qur'ān 2:285–286)

A *ḥadīth* of Prophet Muḥammad ﷺ refers to the above supplications as "two lights" and tells us that our prayers will be answered when we recite them.[76] This is encouraging news for everyone striving hard for Jannah, as the content of these supplications is very meaningful and will help us become among those whom Allāh ﷻ guides and is pleased with, *in shā' Allāh.*

76. See *Ṣaḥīḥ Muslim* (No. 806).

They hasten to do good deeds

"And the forerunners [in faith and good deeds] are the forerunners [in the Hereafter]."

— *Sūrat al-Wāqi'ah* (Qur'ān 56:10)

We mentioned in the introduction to this book that Jannah has different ranks.

Hell-Fire has ranks, too.

But what is the reason behind these ranks?

They exist simply because each person is unique in terms of faith and the nature of his or her deeds (good or bad), so it follows that people will be granted their ranks in the final abode of the Hereafter based on what they have done in the worldly life of this *dunyā*.

"And for all are ranks [i.e., positions resulting] from what they have done."[77]

Allāh ﷻ categorizes the followers of Prophet Muḥammad ﷺ into three categories:[78]

- Those who wrong themselves [they are weak in faith and frequently sin despite their status as believers];
- Those who follow the "middle course" [they are mostly obedient to Allāh but sometimes deviate or fall into sin];
- Those who are (by Allāh's will) foremost in good deeds [they strive for excellence and do not deliberately fall into sin and are filled with remorse when they do].

Here, let us focus on just the final category listed above: **the forerunners**.

The forerunners are those who hasten to do good for the sake of Allāh ﷻ.

They are consistent in their prayers and other obligatory acts of worship while

77. Qur'ān 6:132.

78. Review Qur'ān 35:32.

also following the *sunnah* of the Prophet ﷺ in order to perform numerous voluntary acts of worship as well.

When someone is in need, they are the first ones to help—and they frequently initiate good deeds without the need for a particular occasion or event.

They live their lives as though they are in a race with time to please Allāh ﷻ, and their tongues are moist with *istighfār*,[79] *dhikr*,[80] and supplication.

Despite the above, the forerunners are humble and do not feel proud, as they know that everything they have achieved in this worldly life would not have been possible without the help of Allāh ﷻ Whom they always remember to praise and thank.

The Companions of Prophet Muḥammad ﷺ (may Allāh ﷻ be pleased with them all) were known for always competing with each other in their performance of good deeds. One day, when the Prophet ﷺ commanded the believers to give charity to the poor, 'Umar ibn al-Khaṭṭāb (RA) decided to give away **half of his wealth** in charity, with the thought that this would finally be the day on which he might surpass Abū Bakr al-Ṣiddīq (RA) whom he had never surpassed before in the past. But when Abū Bakr (RA) handed the Prophet ﷺ the amount he had dedicated for charity that day, it turned out that he had brought **all of his wealth** for the sake of Allāh ﷻ. 'Umar ibn al-Khaṭṭāb (RA) then said: "I shall never surpass you in anything."[81]

Allāh ﷻ says that the forerunners are those who are "the nearest" to Him in Jannāt al-Na'īm [The Gardens of Bliss].[82] He also tells us that they are comprised of "a [large] company of the former peoples [from the earlier generations of believers] and a few of the later peoples."[83]

So, why don't we all strive together to be included in this very special class of people whose final abode will be in the highest ranks of Jannah?

79. Seeking pardon from Allāh.

80. Remembrance of Allāh.

81. Refer to *Sunan Abī Dā'ūd* (No. 1678).

82. Qur'ān 56:11–12.

83. Qur'ān 56:13–14.

Don't say it is impossible, as nothing is impossible with effort, *du'ā'*, and the will of Allāh ﷻ.

"Indeed, no one despairs of relief from Allāh except the disbelieving people!"[84]

84. Qur'ān 12:87.

They are kind to their parents

"Our Lord, forgive me and my parents."

— *Sūrat Ibrāhīm* (Qur'ān 14:41)

Allāh ﷻ gives great status to parents and honors them in many ways.

In the Qur'ān, being good to our parents is mentioned alongside the worship of Allāh ﷻ,[85] and we also find that kindness to parents is among the traits of the prophets.[86] Prophet Muḥammad ﷺ has also informed us that kindness to parents is among the actions dearest to Allāh ﷻ.[87]

As shown in the following *ḥadīth*, one of the best everlasting good deeds a person can do for his or her parents that will also raise one's ranks in Jannah is to pray for them—and this is the case whether they are still alive or have already passed away.

"A person will be raised in status in Paradise and say: 'Where did this come from?' And it will be said: 'From your child praying for forgiveness for you.'"[88]

In His great generosity, mercy, and kindness toward His believers, Allāh ﷻ rewards believing parents and children alike by allowing them to be mediators for each other in Jannah so that they may be granted a higher rank there.

"And those who believed and whose descendants followed them in faith - We will join with them their descendants."[89]

This means that individual family members who do not initially reach the same rank together in Jannah will be reunited in the highest rank that any of them reaches!

85. See Qur'ān 17:23.

86. For example, see Qur'ān 19:32.

87. See *Riyāḍ al-Ṣāliḥīn* (No. 1286).

88. A saying of Prophet Muḥammad ﷺ (*Sunan Ibn Mājah*, No. 3660).

89. Qur'ān 52:21.

If you have loved ones who have passed away, don't forget them in your prayers, as they may reach a higher rank in Jannah because of you, and maybe one day they will also be the reason for you to reach a higher rank when you reunite with each other in Jannah, *in shā' Allāh.*

While it is beneficial for us to make *du'ā'* (supplications) in many different circumstances, Prophet Muḥammad ﷺ also advised us that: "The nearest a believer is to his Lord is while he is in prostration, so increase your supplications while prostrating."[90]

Supplications that you can make for your parents include the following ones extracted from the Qur'ān:

- "My Lord, have mercy upon them as they brought me up [when I was] young." (Qur'ān 17:24)
- "My Lord, enable me to be grateful for Your favor which You have bestowed upon me and upon my parents and to work righteousness of which You will approve and make righteous for me my offspring. Indeed, I have repented to You, and indeed, I am of the Muslims." (Qur'ān 46:15)
- "Our Lord, forgive me and my parents and the believers the Day the account is established." (Qur'ān 14:41)

90. *Riyāḍ al-Ṣāliḥīn* (No. 1428).

They Are Persistent and Do Not Give Up

"I wish my people could know."

— *Sūrat Yā-Sīn* (Qur'ān 36:26)

While one could analyze the story associated with this quote in many different ways, one of the main messages I personally derive from it is: **Don't give up**.

Before we delve further into the topic, let us read the story.

A long time ago, in a city where the people did not worship Allāh ﷻ, He sent messengers there to guide them to the right path. But the people of the city denied the messengers and told them that they considered them a "bad omen." They even threatened to stone them and inflict a painful punishment upon them.[91]

A righteous man from the farthest end of the city heard what had happened and advised his people to follow the messengers, saying:[92] "O my people, follow the messengers. Follow those who do not ask of you [any] payment, and they are [rightly] guided."[93]

The people of the city did not appreciate the advice they were offered and unjustly murdered the righteous man.

Then it was said to him: "Enter Paradise [Jannah]," and he said: "I wish my people could know of how my Lord has forgiven me and placed me among the honored."[94]

In a world in which most people are following their desires, it may be a trial for some believers to remain good Muslims, especially if they are the type who are easily influenced by others or find it difficult to withstand the challenges that come with being different.

91. See Qur'ān 36:13–19.

92. See Qur'ān 36:20.

93. Qur'ān 36:20–21.

94. Qur'ān 36:26–27.

In such cases, one should remember that there have always been people who shun goodness and cannot stand the idea of following good advice or changing their lives for the better, and this is often because their bad ways are serving certain interests of theirs. Allāh ﷻ says: "How regretful for [My] servants! There did not come to them any messenger except that they used to ridicule him."[95]

The above story shows the great loss experienced by the wrongdoers in contrast to the immense blessings gained by those who remain steadfast, with an emphasis on the final result being what counts in the end.

Don't give up on being truthful even when the liars are out in full force.

Don't give up on your stance to refrain from backbiting even when the people around you portray it as a bit of harmless fun.

Don't give up on modesty even when it feels like people are giving you unwanted attention because you stand out from the crowd.

Keeping in mind the words of the righteous man in Jannah, make it a daily habit to recite this supplication from the Qur'ān as protection from fluctuations in faith: **"Our Lord, let not our hearts deviate after You have guided us and grant us from Yourself mercy. Indeed, You are the Bestower. Our Lord, surely You will gather the people for a Day about which there is no doubt. Indeed, Allāh does not fail in His promise."**[96]

As one can see, the above story also demonstrates the great importance of being patient and not giving up on wishing goodness for our loved ones. As such, we should always continue to advise the people we care about, even if they happen to deviate from the straight path. Although the man in the above story attained Jannah and no longer had to struggle with the challenges of this *dunyā*, he continued to show concern for his people and wished they could

95. Qur'ān 36:30.
96. Qur'ān 3:8–9.

gain knowledge of the eternal blessings they were missing out on through their rejection of Allāh's guidance.

Although the guidance of a person is in Allāh's hands alone,[97] **we frequently cross paths with certain people in this life by His will,** and this is so that we may be of help to each other by enjoining what is good and advising against what is bad, by being good role models, and by supplicating for each other's guidance. In fact, one can find numerous stories and anecdotes showing how people are positively influenced by other people's prayers and reminders.

A real-life example of this can be seen in the story of a famous singer in the Arab world who recently repented from singing and said that one of the main factors in his decision to repent was a screenshot of a social media post mentioning his name that went viral.

The original post was basically a question asking what this singer "says," and while most people answered with different quotes from the lyrics he used to sing, one of the comments was a bit different and caught his attention, saying that the singer says: "**Oh, I wish I had sent ahead [some good] for my life.**"

This statement is actually a verse from *Sūrat al-Fajr* (Qur'ān 89:24) that talks about those who don't work for their Hereafter—and it was this simple verse that made a huge impact on the former singer, who is now a reciter of the Qur'ān and frequently leads people in prayers at the mosque. He has also said that the support of his mother made a big difference in his decision to remain on the path of goodness.

Never give up on being a good Muslim who acts as a role model to others and reminds them of goodness, as there is no happiness on Earth greater than the happiness that comes with attaining the pleasure of Allāh ﷻ and supporting others in their own journeys to do the same.

97. Qur'ān 28:56.

They regularly renew their good intentions

"Verily, the reward of deeds depends on one's intentions."

— A Saying of Prophet Muḥammad ﷺ *(Sunan Abī Dā'ūd,* No. 2201)

This beautiful saying of our beloved Prophet ﷺ provides extra motivation for anyone striving on the path of Jannah, as we can, with the right intentions, turn every single thing we do in our lives into an act that is pleasing to Allāh ﷻ.

"Even sleeping?"

This was the question posed by one of my classmates when we studied this lesson in school more than ten years ago.

"Even sleeping," answered the teacher, who went on to explain that sleeping with the intention of resting our bodies in order to wake up active the next day for Fajr (morning) prayers is a praiseworthy deed that also results in more productivity as we carry out our other duties for the rest of the day.

Renew your intentions so that everything you do becomes an act intended to please the Creator.

When you are studying, for example, study with the intention of gaining knowledge and benefiting others. When you are working, work with the goal of pleasing Allāh ﷻ (by providing for your family, helping others, and representing Islām). When you visit your relatives, visit them with the intention of following the Islamic teaching of maintaining the ties of kinship. When you give someone a gift, do so with the intention of making it into a form of a secret charity between you and Allāh ﷻ. When you help with the household chores, turn it into an act of worship by purifying your heart and remembering the great rewards that come with maintaining a pleasant living environment for your parents and other family members.

Even when we are engaged in personal hobbies or activities such as exercising, we can add value to them when our intentions are for the sake of Allāh ﷻ. This happens when we show gratitude by taking care of our health and making use of the skills He has blessed us with.

So, brainstorm as many daily activities you can think of, and turn them into deeds that will take you to Jannah, *in shā' Allāh*.

In addition to the above, another *ḥadīth* of the Prophet ﷺ tells us that having the intention of always pleasing Allāh ﷻ also results in one attaining blessings in the worldly life of this *dunyā*!

"Whoever is focused only on this world, Allāh will confound his affairs and make him fear poverty constantly, and he will not get anything of this world except that which has been decreed for him. Whoever is focused on the Hereafter, Allāh will settle his affairs and grant him peace of mind, making him feel content with his lot, and his provision and worldly gains will come to him regardless (of circumstances, obstacles, or people)."[98]

98. *Sunan Ibn Mājah* (No. 4105).

They are allies to Allāh ﷻ

"And He will be their protecting friend."

— *Sūrat al-An'ām* (Qur'ān 6:127)

This protecting friend is Allāh ﷻ!

Allāh ﷻ tells us that He has displayed the straight path in front of us and detailed all of the signs that allow us to recognize the truth, yet only those who reason will be the ones to follow,[99] and these are the people to whom Allāh ﷻ will be a protecting friend. "**For them will be the Abode of Peace [Jannah] with their Lord. And He will be their protecting friend because of what they used to do.**"[100]

It will be their protecting friend and guardian (Allāh ﷻ) Who forgives them and conceals their sins on the Day when nothing is concealed, because they will have lived in this *dunyā* as **allies of Allāh** ﷻ, having both faith and *taqwá*, and doing their best to be among the righteous as Allāh ﷻ loves.

Some descriptions of the allies of Allāh ﷻ include the following:

- They follow Allāh's guidance (Qur'ān 2:38);
- They submit in Islām to Allāh ﷻ (Qur'ān 2:112);
- They are doers of good (Qur'ān 2:112);
- They give charity for the sake of Allāh ﷻ, without constantly reminding people of their generosity (Qur'ān 2:262);
- They are humble (Qur'ān 25:63);
- When the ignorant address them harshly, they only say words of peace (Qur'ān 25:63);
- They constantly repent (Qur'ān 25:70);

99. Qur'ān 6:126.
100. Qur'ān 6:127.

- They do not testify to falsehood (Qur'ān 25:72);
- When they pass by idle [frivolous] talk, they pass by with dignity (Qur'ān 25:72);
- When they are reminded of the verses of their Lord, they do not fall upon them deaf and blind (Qur'ān 25:73).

These are the people whom Allāh ﷻ tells us "will be awarded the Chamber[101] for what they patiently endured, and they will be received therein with greetings and [words of] peace, abiding eternally therein. What an excellent place to settle and reside!"[102]

Among the blessings Allāh ﷻ grants His righteous allies as a sign of His pleasure with them in the temporary life of this *dunyā* are spiritual gifts known in Arabic as *karāmāt*. Unlike miracles, which are only granted to prophets, *karāmāt* are a means of providing support to the righteous in specific circumstances.

It could be something like answering their supplications or providing them with tranquility or helping them out of a distressing situation.

There are several authentic stories about righteous individuals attaining *karāmāt* from Allāh ﷻ. One such story involves three men who got trapped in a cave that they had taken shelter in from the rain when a huge rock fell down from the mountain and blocked the entrance.

They told each other that the only way out of this calamity would be to make sincere supplications by virtue of the good deeds they had done in their lives purely for the sake of Allāh ﷻ.

One of them told a story about treating his parents with kindness and respect, even while they were asleep, while the second spoke of refraining from the sin of fornication during a moment of extreme weakness.

---

101. The most elevated portion of Paradise.
102. Qur'ān 25:75–76.

The third talked about investing the wages of a worker who did not come on time to receive his payment, later giving him all of the profits from the investment without keeping anything for himself. Each time one of the men told his story, the rock would move a little, until the last one finished his story, and the entrance became wide enough for them to pass through.[103]

This is but one example of the many secret blessings experienced by those who are close to Allāh ﷻ in this life and continuously strive for Jannah, which is very different from the blessings granted after hardship to people who are astray and do not repent from their evil ways. Such blessings are for an entirely different purpose, as can be seen clearly in the verses Allāh ﷻ has revealed to us about some of the older nations who were allies of Satan:

"And We have already sent [messengers] to nations before you, [O Muḥammad]; then We seized them with poverty and hardship that perhaps they might humble themselves [to Us]. Then why, when Our punishment came to them, did they not humble themselves? But their hearts became hardened, and Satan made attractive to them that which they were doing. So when they forgot that by which they had been reminded,[104] **We opened to them the doors of every [good] thing** until, when they rejoiced in that which they were given, We seized them suddenly, and they were [then] in despair."[105]

Never forget that Allāh's protective friendship is granted **only** to His allies who follow His teachings and embody the traits of a true believer in this life. "Indeed, Allāh defends those who have believed. Indeed, Allāh does not like anyone treacherous and ungrateful."[106]

103. This story was told by Prophet Muḥammad ﷺ (see *Riyāḍ al-Ṣāliḥīn*, No. 12).

104. Deliberately disregarding what the messengers had told them.

105. Qur'ān 6:42–44.

106. Qur'ān 22:38.

They are moderate in spending money

"But are ever, between that, [justly] moderate."

— *Sūrat al-Furqān* (Qur'ān 25:67)

Allāh ﷻ further describes the people whom He is pleased with as "**those who, when they spend, do so not excessively or sparingly but are ever, between that, [justly] moderate.**"[107]

Such people have understood that any money in our possession is actually a test, as we will be asked where we got it from and how we spent it—and we will also be held accountable for misusing it, because it is one of the provisions Allāh ﷻ has entrusted us with on this earth.

While Islām places great emphasis on dedicating a portion of our wealth for charity, it also teaches us to be moderate in terms of how we otherwise spend the money we have been blessed with—and this is achieved by first establishing priorities, which helps us budget for essential needs and other expenses.

Secondly, a believer should exercise a certain amount of discipline and self-restraint when it comes to spending.

Being disciplined with money is not stinginess as some may wrongly believe. It is instead freeing ourselves from the shackles of materialism, as unrestrained spending leads to excessiveness, and Allāh ﷻ "**does not like those who commit excess.**"[108]

If you are the type of person who is content with simplicity and does not chase after the luxuries of this world, you are truly blessed.

107. Qur'ān 25:67.
108. Qur'ān 7:31.

Prophet Muḥammad ﷺ summarized this peaceful state of mind with the following words:

"Whoever among you wakes up physically healthy, feeling safe and secure within himself, with food for the day, it is as if he acquired the whole world."[109]

During 'Umar ibn al-Khaṭṭāb's reign as caliph, the Islamic nation expanded as the Muslims reached a number of new lands with the message of Islām, and this was a great victory and blessing from Allāh ﷻ from a spiritual perspective, because a new era free from injustice and corruption was finally about to begin, based on the teachings of the Creator ﷻ.

Whenever a new land was liberated, 'Umar (RA) would send letters to the newly appointed leaders with Islamic advice and reminders not to become too attached to the worldly provisions they had attained through their positions as rulers over the people. Among the things he said was: "Beware of comfort [or luxury] and the dress of the polytheists and the wearing of silk garments."[110]

Some people may not realize that the sudden blessings of wealth and comfort after a long period of hardship may actually cause one's faith to weaken or deteriorate if one is not careful and vigilant. As such, 'Umar (RA) was keen on reminding the Muslims not to forget that true victory lies in attaining the treasures of the Hereafter.

In the Qur'ān, Allāh ﷻ tells us the story of Qārūn, who was a wealthy man from the nation of Mūsá (Moses) (PBUH). Although Qārūn was given an abundance of blessings from His Lord, he was not thankful to Allāh ﷻ, and was instead among the corrupters of his land.

Those who were weak in faith and desired the life of this world used to admire his riches and would feel envious whenever they saw Qārūn appear before them in his adornment. They would say: "Oh, would that we had like what was given to Qārūn. Indeed, he is one of great fortune."

---

109. *Sunan Ibn Mājah* (No. 4141).
110. *Ṣaḥīḥ Muslim* (No. 2069).

Those with stronger faith, however, knew that Qārūn was instead on the path to great misfortune. This is why they would advise those who were deluded by Qārūn's way of life, saying: "Woe to you! The reward of Allāh is better for he who believes and does righteousness. And none are granted it except the patient."

The pious among them advised Qārūn himself against his arrogant ways, saying: "Do not exult. Indeed, Allāh does not like the exultant. **But seek, through that which Allāh has given you, the home of the Hereafter; and [yet], do not forget your share of the world. And do good as Allāh has done good to you. And desire not corruption in the land.** Indeed, Allāh does not like corrupters."

But Qārūn paid no heed to this wise advice and instead arrogantly claimed that his wealth had been given to him due to some knowledge he had.

It was just a matter of time before Qārūn faced a horrendous punishment for his evil deeds as the earth swallowed up both Qārūn and his home, rendering him helpless with no one able to come to his aid.

Seeing what happened to him, the people who had been admiring Qārūn's wealth realized how mistaken they had been and said: "Oh, how Allāh extends provision to whom He wills of His servants and restricts it! If not that Allāh had conferred favor on us, He would have caused it [i.e., the earth] to swallow us. Oh, how the disbelievers do not succeed!"

At the conclusion of this story, Allāh ﷻ tells us: "**That [eternal] home of the Hereafter [in Jannah] We assign to those who do not desire exaltedness upon the earth or corruption. And the [best] outcome is for the righteous.**"[111]

111. For the whole story, review Qur'ān 28:76–83.

Their hearts are sound

"But only one who comes to Allāh with a sound heart."

— *Sūrat al-Shuʿarāʾ* (Qur'ān 26:89)

One day, Prophet Muḥammad ﷺ told some of his Companions (may Allāh ﷻ be pleased with them) about a certain man whom he said would be among the inhabitants of Jannah. One of them decided to stay at the man's house to see what special acts of worship he was doing so that he could be like him. Without revealing his true reason, the Companion asked the man if he could stay with him for a few days, and he allowed him to do so. But after observing him for a while, the Companion was surprised to see that man was a very ordinary person; he did not spend long nights in prayer, nor did he spend his days engaged in extra acts of worship beyond the minimum required of a practicing Muslim.

So, he finally decided to ask the man what his secret was, and the man told him: "It is not but as you see, except that I find no malice within myself toward the Muslims, nor do I envy anyone for the good that Allāh has given him."[112]

This is a description of someone with a sound heart.

It is essential for us to stand before the Creator on the Day of Resurrection with a sound heart, as Jannah will be brought forth to the righteous on that day so that they may enter it by the will and mercy of Allāh ﷻ.[113]

While there are surely many different ways to describe the qualities associated with a sound heart, we can comfortably say that someone with a sound heart:

- Believes in Allāh ﷻ and does not associate partners with Him;

112. As found in *Musnad Aḥmad*.
113. Qur'ān 26:90.

- Does not harbor hatred, envy, or jealousy toward others;
- Is generally kind, loving, and pardoning;
- Does not hold grudges;
- Is moved and comforted by the remembrance of Allāh ﷻ.

We can train ourselves to attain such qualities by:

- Making sincere supplications to Allāh ﷻ;
- Committing to the five obligatory prayers;
- Reading the Qur'ān on a regular basis and studying the meanings of the verses;
- Smiling to others and greeting them with words "al-salāmu 'alaykum" (peace be upon you), as taught to us by the Prophet ﷺ;
- Dealing with people based on what is apparent without delving too deeply into their true intentions so long as they are not causing overt harm;
- Finding excuses for others in times of disappointment;
- Refraining from gossip and backbiting;
- Generally keeping ourselves busy with beneficial things.

To maintain the purity of our hearts, Prophet Muḥammad ﷺ advised us to say this supplication in the morning, in the evening, and whenever we go to sleep:

"O Allāh, Knower of the Unseen and the Visible, Creator of the heavens and the earth, everything is in Your hands. I testify that there is no god but You. I seek refuge with You from the evil of myself and the evil of Satan and his (encouragement to) associate others (with You) (in worship)."[114]

114. *al-Adab al-Mufrad* (No. 1202).

Allāh ﷻ tells us that any blemishes in the heart, such as jealousy and envy, will be effortlessly removed in the Hereafter so that the believers sit facing each other as brothers.[115] This shows that even those destined for Jannah are not completely free of such emotions in the worldly life of this *dunyā*, which means that we must be aware of this test and continuously work on refining our character while we still have the opportunity to do so.

115. See Qur'ān 15:47.

They Choose Their Companions Carefully

"And when the souls are paired."

— *Sūrat al-Takwīr* (Qur'ān 81:7)

Keep in mind that we will be gathered on the Day of Resurrection with those who are like us (in faith, morals, and deeds).

This is why it is very important to choose the people we are surrounded with in this *dunyā* carefully, because it is almost guaranteed that we will unconsciously adopt the ethics and morals of our close friends.

Allāh ﷻ tells us that on the Day of Judgment close friends "will be enemies to each other, except for the righteous,"[116] who will enter Jannah together, along with their "kinds."[117] Allāh ﷻ promises that such people will be granted "whatever the souls desire and [what] delights the eyes" in Paradise as a reward for their good deeds.[118]

Someone who befriends bad people, on the other hand, will be let down in the Hereafter. In regret, he will say: "Oh, woe to me! I wish I had not taken so-and-so as a friend. He led me away from the remembrance [of Allāh] after it had come to me. And ever is Satan, to man, a deserter."[119]

Never choose anyone over your *dīn*, religion, and faith, as this means following the path of Satan, and Satan will let the people who listen to him down twice—first when he diverts them from the path of goodness in this *dunyā*, causing them the distress of being misguided, and second in this scene in the Hereafter:

"And Satan will say when the matter has been concluded: 'Indeed, Allāh had promised you the promise of truth. And I promised you, but I betrayed you.

116. See Qur'ān 43:67.
117. See Qur'ān 43:70.
118. See Qur'ān 43:71–72.
119. Qur'ān 25:28–29.

But I had no authority over you except that I invited you, and you responded to me. So do not blame me; but blame yourselves. I cannot be called to your aid, nor can you be called to my aid. Indeed, I deny your association of me [with Allāh] before. Indeed, for the wrongdoers is a painful punishment.'"[120]

Some of the qualities associated with genuinely good friends include the following:

- They are truthful (Qur'ān 9:119);
- They advise each other to truth and patience (Qur'ān 103:3);
- They enjoin what is good and advise against what is sinful (Qur'ān9:71);
- They observe their prayers and practice *zakāt* (obligatory charity) (Qur'ān 9:71);
- They obey Allāh ﷻ (Qur'ān 9:71).

In the below verse from *Sūrat al-Kahf*, Allāh ﷻ brings attention to the importance of surrounding oneself with righteous company and staying away from bad company in order to remain on the right path:

"And keep yourself patient [by being] with those who call upon their Lord in the morning and the evening, seeking His face [i.e., acceptance]. And let not your eyes pass beyond them, desiring adornments of the worldly life, and do not obey one whose heart We have made heedless of Our remembrance and who follows his desire and whose affair is ever [in] neglect [by disobeying Allāh ﷻ]."[121]

120. Qur'ān 14:22.
121. Qur'ān 18:28.

They are devoted to the Qur'ān

"Your rank will be at the last *āyah* (verse) you recite."

— A Saying of Prophet Muḥammad ﷺ (*Riyāḍ al-Ṣāliḥīn*, No. 1001)

While friendships are sometimes fleeting and come to an end for one reason or another in the worldly life of this *dunyā*, there is one companion that one should never abandon regardless of the circumstance, and that is the Qur'ān, which shall remain as devoted to you as you are to it and will never disappoint you or let you down.

The Prophet ﷺ said: "**Someone who was devoted to the Qur'ān [in this life] will be told on the Day of Resurrection: 'Recite and ascend [in ranks] as you used to recite when you were in the *dunyā*. Your rank [in Jannah] will be at the last *āyah* (verse) you recite.'**"[122]

This means that the more effort you put into reading, reciting, and learning the Qur'ān, the higher your rank in Jannah will be.

Why is that?

Because it is a Book of Guidance revealed from the Heavens to light the path for us in this *dunyā*—and someone who holds on to this light cannot ever go wrong. The Glorious Qur'ān was never meant as a book to be set aside and used only on special occasions; rather, it is meant to continually illuminate our hearts and minds.

It is a provider of patience in times of difficulty or turmoil.

It is a healer of negativity, bad habits, and undesirable traits.

It is a record of truth and true guidance.

It is a giver of hope.

---

122. *Riyāḍ al-Ṣāliḥīn* (No. 1001).

It is a remedy for all forms of sadness and stress.

It is a reminder of who Allāh ﷻ, our Creator, actually is.

The Qur'ān is a gift with a message for all of humanity, and not just Muslims, to guide us on the journey of life so that we are able to recognize the path of righteousness and make the best choices along the way.

In a passage from *Sūrat al-Mā'idah*, Allāh ﷻ specifically addresses the Christians and Jews, telling them:

"O People of the Scripture, there has come to you Our Messenger making clear to you much of what you used to conceal of the Scripture and overlooking much. There has come to you from Allāh a light and a clear Book [the Qur'ān] by which Allāh guides those who pursue His pleasure to the ways of peace[123] and brings them out from darknesses into the light, by His permission, and guides them to a straight path."[124]

He also tells us that the true believers from other religions will realize that they were already Muslims when they hear the Qur'ān:

"And when it is recited to them, they say: 'We have believed in it; indeed, it is the truth from our Lord. Indeed we were, [even] before it, Muslims [i.e., submitting to Allāh].'"[125]

Allāh ﷻ promises that such people "will be given their reward twice for what they patiently endured, and [because] they repel evil with good."[126]

Make the best use of Allāh's precious gift to humankind as the Companions of Prophet Muḥammad ﷺ used to do. It is narrated that they viewed the verses of the Qur'ān as messages from their Lord, reflecting upon them at night, and acting upon them during the day,[127] and this is what made them the best of all nations.

123. Freedom from all evil.

124. Qur'ān 5:15–16.

125. Qur'ān 28:53.

126. Qur'ān 28:54.

127. As found in *al-Tibyān fī Ādāb Ḥamalat al-Qur'ān.*

If you are striving to develop the habit of reading the Qur'ān on a daily basis, here are some tips that may help:

- Stick to a specific time every day, preferably after the dawn prayer of Ṣalāt al-Fajr, as Allāh ﷻ tells us: **"Indeed, the recitation of dawn is ever witnessed,"**[128] meaning that the angels of both daytime and nighttime witness our Fajr (morning) prayers, making it a time of increased blessings.
- Consider it something mandatory that cannot be missed.
- Set short-term practical goals that you can achieve without feeling overwhelmed.
- Focus on the quality of your reading rather than on the quantity, as the goal is to fully absorb Allāh's words.
- Make sure that you have easy access to the Qur'ān (on a mobile app, for example).

Prophet Muḥammad ﷺ said: "Read the Qur'ān, for it will come as an intercessor for its reciters on the Day of Resurrection."[129]

Whether it is a page, a chapter, or even just a single verse, any effort that you put into reading and learning the Qur'ān will definitely make a difference to your status in the Hereafter.

Allāh ﷻ tells us many times to read the Qur'ān, as found in the following verses:

"Recite what is easy [for you] of the Qur'ān." (Qur'ān 73:20)

"Then do they not reflect upon the Qur'ān, or are there locks upon [their] hearts?" (Qur'ān 47:24)

128. Qur'ān 17:78; also see *Ṣaḥīḥ al-Bukhārī* (No. 648).
129. *Riyāḍ al-Ṣāliḥīn* (No. 991).

"And recite, what has been revealed to you of the Book of your Lord. There is no changer of His words, and never will you find in other than Him a refuge."

(Qur'ān 18:27)

THEY LIVE BY THE LIGHT OF THE QUR'ĀN

"And turn to Allāh in repentance, all of you, O believers, that you might succeed."

— *Sūrat al-Nūr* (Qur'ān 24:31)

Living by the Qur'ān's light means changing your entire lifestyle so that you are living according to Allāh's teachings.

Many of the verses found in *Sūrat al-Nūr* (the literal meaning of which is "The Chapter of Light") contain teachings and laws to regulate a Muslim's life.

This chapter of the Qur'ān mentions the prohibition of fornication and adultery. It also emphasizes modesty for both genders and the need to ask for permission when visiting people in their homes.

This is also where the "verse of light" (Qur'ān 24:35) can be found, informing us about the light of Allāh ﷻ, which is the purest of all lights. Other verses in *Sūrat al-Nūr* remind us of repentance, helping us understand that the true spirit of repentance is not just a matter of seeking Allāh's forgiveness for any sins one has committed, but instead requires us to implement genuine improvements to our behavior and morals—sometimes making radical changes to our entire outlook on life and way of living.

Depending on the circumstances, it may be extremely difficult at times for someone to make such changes, especially when it becomes necessary to leave behind any undesirable habits and beliefs one has been raised with—but this is indeed the way to success, which is why Allāh ﷻ tells us that turning to Him in repentance is for one's own benefit, "so that you may succeed."[130]

130. Qur'ān 24:31. Another translation of this verse says "so that [you] may attain Bliss," in reference to the eternal bliss of Paradise, which is where true success lies.

This is the only way to attain the light of Allāh's guidance.

Having knowledge about the path of guidance yet deliberately choosing to follow the path of desires, on the other hand, results in great loss as Allāh ﷻ tells us in the following passage from *Sūrat al-A'rāf*:

"And recite to them, [O Muḥammad], the news of him[131] to whom We gave [knowledge of] Our signs, but he detached himself from them; so Satan pursued him, and he became of the deviators.[132] And if We had willed, We could have elevated him thereby, but he adhered [instead] to the earth[133] and followed his own desire. So his example is like that of the dog: if you chase him, he pants, or if you leave him, he [still] pants. That is the example of the people who denied Our signs. So relate the stories that perhaps they will give thought."[134]

Allāh ﷻ also tells us about the later generations who neglected the right path: "But there came after them successors [later generations] who neglected prayer and pursued desires; so they are going to meet evil [consequences], except those who repent, believe and do righteousness; for those will enter Paradise and will not be wronged at all."[135]

Allāh ﷻ shows us in such verses that the opportunity to attain Jannah as our final abode in the Hereafter is always present so long as we are still alive in this *dunyā*. It does not matter who we are or what background or ethnicity we come from. Allāh ﷻ is our Creator and knows that we are not perfect and all have many shortcomings as flawed human beings who are facing many tests and struggles in this life. But believers are different from others in that they maintain awareness of their faults and are always striving to make positive changes, which includes repenting to Allāh ﷻ and working to replace their sins with good deeds.

131. A man from Banī Isrā'īl at the time of Prophet Mūsá (Moses) (PBUH).

132. Persisting in falsehood to the point of destruction.

133. Worldly temptations.

134. Qur'ān 7:175–176.

135. Qur'ān 19:59–60.

Let this provide motivation for all of us to scrutinize the areas of our lives in which we don't follow the teachings of Allāh ﷻ as well as we should so that we may attempt to fix them.

They Maintain the Light of Faith

"Our Lord, perfect for us our light."

— *Sūrat al-Taḥrīm* (Qur'ān 66:8)

Those who are sincere about attaining the light of Allāh's guidance in this *dunyā*, continuously repenting and humbling themselves to Allāh ﷻ, will be seen on the Day of Judgment with their light glowing in the darkness:

"On the Day you see the believing men and believing women, their light proceeding before them and on their right."[136]

The hypocrites,[137] on the other hand (as mentioned in some explanations of the related verse that are based on a saying of Prophet Muḥammad ﷺ),[138] will have lights with them that will suddenly dim out and die, which is a sign that they will not be able to enter Jannah. This is when the true believers will say to their Lord: **"Our Lord, perfect for us our light and forgive us. Indeed, You are over all things competent."**[139]

Allāh ﷻ says He will not disgrace the believers or let them down; rather, He will remove from them their misdeeds,[140] and it will be said to them: "'Your good tidings today are [of] gardens beneath which rivers flow, wherein you will abide eternally.' That is indeed the great attainment."[141]

And this is how their lights are perfected, when they are finally allowed to enter Jannah.

As the believers carry their light with them on their way to Jannah, the hypocrites will say to them: "Wait for us [so] that we may acquire some of your light."[142]

---

136. Qur'ān 57:12.

137. The hypocrites are those who appear to be Muslims on the surface, but are actually enemies of Islām who conceal their intent to cause harm to Muslim society. The Prophet ﷺ said: "There are three signs of a hypocrite: when he speaks, he lies; when he makes a promise, he breaks it; and when he is entrusted, he betrays his trust." (*Ṣaḥīḥ al-Bukhārī*, No. 33.)

138. See *Ṣaḥīḥ Muslim* (No. 191a).

139. Qur'ān 66:8.

140. See Qur'ān 66:8.

141. Qur'ān 57:12.

142. Qur'ān 57:13.

At this point, they will be told: "Go back behind you and seek light!"[143]

But this will not be possible, as light is only acquired in the worldly life of this *dunyā* and cannot be obtained once a person has exited this life.

A wall will then be erected between the true believers and the hypocrites, preventing the hypocrites from entering Paradise. In a state of desperation, the hypocrites will start calling out to the believers: "Were we not with you [living as Muslims in the *dunyā*]?"[144]

The believers will say: "Yes, but you afflicted yourselves [with hypocrisy] and awaited [misfortune for us] and doubted, and wishful thinking deluded you until there came the command of Allāh. And the Deceiver [i.e., Satan] deceived you concerning Allāh. So today no ransom will be taken from you or from those who disbelieved. Your refuge is the Fire. It is most worthy of you, and wretched is the destination."[145]

Some descriptions of the hypocrites found in the Qur'ān include the following:

- They are liars (Qur'ān 63:1);
- They are arrogant (Qur'ān 63:5);
- They dislike spending (Qur'ān 63:7);
- They stand lazily in prayer and only pray for the sake of people (Qur'ān 4:142);
- They barely remember Allāh ﷻ (Qur'ān 4:142);
- They "waver" between faith and disbelief (Qur'ān 4:143);

142. Qur'ān 57:13.
143. Qur'ān 57:13.
144. Qur'ān 57:14.
145. Qur'ān 57:14–15.

- They are cowards (Qur'ān 9:57);
- They mock everything related to Islām (Qur'ān 9:64–65).

In a verse from *Sūrat al-Ḥadīd*, Allāh ﷻ tells us: "Has the time not come for those who have believed that their hearts should become humbly submissive at the remembrance of Allāh and what has come down of the truth? And let them not be like those who were given the Scripture before, and a long period passed over them, so their hearts hardened; and many of them are defiantly disobedient."[146]

He also tells us: "Know that Allāh gives life to the earth after its lifelessness. We have made clear to you the signs; perhaps you will understand."[147]

This verse gives hope regarding those who have gone astray, showing that their hearts may one day be softened in the same manner that the earth comes to life after being lifeless. **If someone has gone down a wrong path** that is displeasing to Allāh ﷻ, this does not mean that this person is doomed to continue on the same path for the rest of his or her days. Recognize, first of all, that Allāh ﷻ has given us the means to attain guidance wherever we are. His signs are all around us like guideposts that can take us from darkness into the light, but we must also be brave enough to take the initiative to change direction when needed before it is too late.

"Indeed, the hypocrites will be in the lowest depths of the Fire—and never will you find for them a helper—**except for those who repent, correct themselves, hold fast to Allāh, and are sincere in their religion for Allāh**, for those will be with the believers. And Allāh is going to give the believers a great reward."[148]

146. Qur'ān 57:16.
147. Qur'ān 57:17.
148. Qur'ān 4:145–146.

THEY CULTIVATE A SPECIAL RELATIONSHIP WITH ALLĀH ﷻ

"My Lord, build for me near You a house in Paradise (Jannah)."

— *Sūrat al-Taḥrīm* (Qur'ān 66:11)

Those who are destined for Jannah have a very special relationship with Allāh ﷻ in the worldly life of this *dunyā*. They think good of Him and do not hesitate to call upon Him at any time of the day or night, because they are certain of His love and concern for them despite their imperfections and shortcomings.

This special relationship with Allāh ﷻ through our supplications (*du'ā'*) can be achieved by implementing the obedience required of us in the following verse of the Qur'ān:

"And when My servants ask you, [O Muḥammad], concerning Me - indeed I am near. I respond to the invocation of the supplicant when he calls upon Me. So let them respond to Me [by obedience] and believe in Me that they may be [rightly] guided."[149]

Some of the etiquettes associated with making supplications to Allāh ﷻ are:

- Showing respect and devotion when addressing Allāh ﷻ;[150]
- Starting the *du'ā'* by praising Allāh ﷻ and acknowledging His great knowledge and power that cannot be compared to ours;[151]
- Having confidence in Allāh's wisdom in managing our affairs, as it may happen that the things we have asked for do not come to pass—yet we should not be disappointed, as the matter will either take time or be reserved as an extra reward in the Hereafter.[152]

149. Qur'ān 2:186.
150. See Qur'ān 98:5.
151. See *Jāmi' al-Tirmidhī* (No. 3476).
152. See *Musnad Aḥmad* (No. 11133).

The Qur'ān presents many different examples of various supplications that can be said in different situations, showing us how one's sincere supplication leads to Jannah.

For example, Allāh ﷻ has told us about those "**who remember Allāh while standing or sitting or [lying] on their sides and give thought to the creation of the heavens and the earth**"[153] while making heartfelt supplications such as the following:

- "Our Lord, You did not create this[154] aimlessly; exalted are You [above such a thing]; so protect us from the punishment of the Fire." (Qur'ān 3:191)
- "Our Lord, indeed we have heard a caller [Prophet Muḥammad (ﷺ)] calling to faith, [saying], 'Believe in your Lord,' and we have believed. Our Lord, so forgive us our sins and remove from us our misdeeds and cause us to die among the righteous." (Qur'ān 3:193)
- "Our Lord, and grant us what You promised us through Your messengers and do not disgrace us on the Day of Resurrection. Indeed, You do not fail in [Your] promise." (Qur'ān 3:194)

Allāh ﷻ provides comfort for the people who have made such supplications, saying:

- "**Never will I allow to be lost the work of [any] worker among you, whether male or female.**" (Qur'ān 3:195)
- "**I will surely remove from them their misdeeds, and I will surely admit them to gardens beneath which rivers flow as reward from Allāh, and Allāh has with Him the best reward.**" (Qur'ān 3:195)

153. Qur'ān 3:191.
154. Referring to the heavens and the earth.

They maintain their remembrance of Allāh ﷻ

"[By] men whom neither commerce nor sale distracts from the remembrance of Allāh."

— *Sūrat al-Nūr* (Qur'ān 24:37)

Those destined for Jannah in the Hereafter strive for balance in their worldly lives.

They may have jobs and other interests they are devoted to in this *dunyā*, but this does not cause them to neglect their prayers, their Islamic morals, and their overall devotion to Allāh ﷻ.

This is because they know that Allāh's magnificent rewards for His pious servants in the Hereafter are everlasting and thus far superior to the temporary diversions of this life.

It once happened that Prophet Muḥammad ﷺ was delivering the sermon during Friday prayers when a trade caravan full of supplies arrived in Madīnah. Some of the Muslims became impatient when they saw it and rushed to see the new merchandise, leaving the Prophet ﷺ to stand alone at the pulpit.[155] Allāh ﷻ then revealed this verse from *Sūrat al-Jumuʿah*: "**What is with Allāh is better than [any] amusement or trade, and Allāh is the best of providers.**"[156]

Another verse states that one should abandon trade and "proceed to the remembrance of Allāh" when the *adhān* is called for Friday prayers, as "that is better for you, if you only knew."[157] Once the prayer has been concluded, however, Allāh ﷻ tells us: "Disperse within the land and seek from the bounty of Allāh, and remember Allāh often **that you may succeed.**"[158]

155. Review Qur'ān 62:11.

156. Qur'ān 62:11.

157. Qur'ān 62:9.

158. Qur'ān 62:10.

These verses show that a Muslim should always give due importance to the obligatory acts of worship, just as we do to our worldly affairs.

A university student, for example, should strive to maintain all of his or her prayers, taking advantage of any breaks between lectures. Likewise, a businessperson or company employee should also make time for obligatory prayers no matter how busy things may get at work. The same goes for stay-at-home parents and all others. No matter who we are, we should not neglect praying on time despite our many duties and responsibilities.

Allāh ﷻ has told us that He will reward those who do not allow their worldly affairs to distract them from the remembrance of Him "**[according to] the best of their deeds** and increase them from His bounty, [for] Allāh gives provision to whom He wills without account [limit],"[159] which is a clear reference to the great reward of Jannah.

While the remembrance of Allāh ﷻ can take many forms, some *dhikr* from the Qur'ān that we can say throughout the day includes the following verses and supplications:

- "Our Lord, give us in this world [that which is] good and in the Hereafter [that which is] good and protect us from the punishment of the Fire." (Qur'ān 2:201)
- "Our Lord, forgive us our sins and the excess [committed] in our affairs." (Qur'ān 3:147)
- "And appoint for us from Yourself a protector and appoint for us from Yourself a helper." (Qur'ān 4:75)
- "And provide for us, and You are the best of providers." (Qur'ān 5:114)
- "Our Lord, pour upon us patience and let us die as Muslims [in submission to You]." (Qur'ān 7:126)

159. Qur'ān 24:38.

- "My Lord, cause me to enter a sound entrance and to exit a sound exit and grant me from Yourself a supporting authority." (Qur'ān 17:80)
- "My Lord, expand [i.e., relax] for me my breast [with assurance], and ease for me my task, and untie the knot from my tongue that they may understand my speech." (Qur'ān 20:25–28)
- "My Lord, increase me in knowledge." (Qur'ān 20:114)
- "My Lord, save me from the wrongdoing people." (Qur'ān 28:21)
- "Sufficient for me is Allāh; there is no deity except Him. On Him I have relied, and He is the Lord of the Great Throne." (Qur'ān 9:129)

Keeping the tongue moist with such phrases helps us remember the Creator in every situation. We also find the following supplications and words of *dhikr* in the authentic *sunnah* of Prophet Muḥammad ﷺ:

- "I seek the forgiveness of Allāh; there is no true god except Allāh, the Ever-Living, the Self- Subsisting, and I turn to Him in repentance." (*Riyāḍ al-Ṣāliḥīn*, No. 1874)
- "[All] praise is due to Allāh Who fed us, provided us drink, satisfied us, and gave us protection." (*Ṣaḥīḥ Muslim*, No. 2715)
- "O Allāh, I seek refuge in you from grief and sadness, from weakness and laziness, from miserliness and cowardice, from being overcome by debt, and from being overpowered by others." (*Ḥiṣn al-Muslim*, No. 121)
- "O Allāh! I seek refuge in You from the evil of that which I have done and the evil of that which I have not done." (*Riyāḍ al-Ṣāliḥīn*, No. 1477)
- "O Allāh, I seek Your forgiveness and Your protection in this world and in the Hereafter." (*Ḥiṣn al-Muslim*, No. 84)

They Dedicate Time at Night for Prayer

"And pray at night when others are asleep."

— A Saying of Prophet Muḥammad ﷺ (*Riyāḍ al-Ṣāliḥīn*, No. 1166)

In a passage from *Sūrat al-Dhāriyāt*, Allāh ﷻ tells us: "Indeed, the righteous will be among gardens and springs, accepting what their Lord has given them. Indeed, they were before that doers of good. They used to sleep but little of the night [spending it in the remembrance of Allāh ﷻ], and in the hours before dawn they would ask forgiveness."[160]

The love such people have for The Creator in the worldly life of this *dunyā* makes them want to spend even more time with Him beyond the ordinary prayers one offers during the day—and this is why they can frequently be found dedicating some time away from the hustle and bustle of everyday life to connect with Him privately in the silence of the night.

This was also the practice of Prophet Muḥammad ﷺ, who gave us this advice: "O people, spread greetings (of peace), feed (the poor and needy) and **pray at night** when others are asleep so that you may enter Jannah in peace."[161]

As narrated by the Prophet's wife 'Ā'ishah (RA): "The Prophet ﷺ would stand (in prayer) so long that the skin of his feet would crack. I ('Ā'ishah) asked him: 'Why do you do this while your past and future sins have been forgiven (as a prophet)?' He said: 'Should I not be a grateful servant of Allāh?'"[162]

In an age when it has become the norm for many to stay up late at night engaged in non-spiritual pursuits, such as browsing social media, watching movies, and going out with friends, it is crucial that we put some thought into assessing how we use these precious hours that may help turn one into a grateful servant of Allāh ﷻ who enters Jannah in a state of peace.

160. Qur'ān 51:15–18.
161. *Riyāḍ al-Ṣāliḥīn* (No. 1166).
162. *Riyāḍ al-Ṣāliḥīn* (No. 98).

With this in mind, let's make it a goal to forgo some of our favorite "worldly" activities in favor of performing Qiyām al-Layl (night prayers) every once in a while in order to improve our relationship with Allāh ﷻ. Even if one's habit is usually only to sleep at night, waking up for such prayers shows dedication to Allāh ﷻ, which can only result in increased blessings in the life of a believer, such as the following:

- Having one's supplications answered;[163]
- Attaining the love of Allāh ﷻ;[164]
- Attaining the highest ranks of Jannah.[165]

163. As found in *Ṣaḥīḥ Muslim* (No. 757).
164. See *Ṣaḥīḥ Muslim* (No. 1159).
165. See *Musnad Aḥmad* (No. 6615).

They perfect their wuḍū' (ablutions)

"Performing the *wuḍū'* properly in spite of difficult circumstances."

— A Saying of Prophet Muḥammad ﷺ (*Riyāḍ al-Ṣāliḥīn*, No. 1059)

Wuḍū' is the Arabic word for the ablutions (ritual washing) one does in preparation for the Islamic prayer—and perfecting it is a means for one to attain a higher rank in Jannah.

It is reported that the Prophet ﷺ said: "Shall I not tell you something by which Allāh effaces the sins and elevates the ranks (in Jannah)?"

The Companions (may Allāh ﷻ be pleased with them) said: "Yes (please tell us), O Messenger of Allāh."

He said, **"Performing the *wuḍū'* properly in spite of difficult circumstances...."**[166]

The Prophet ﷺ has also told us that the *wuḍū'* will be among the distinguishing features of the believers in the Hereafter, saying: "My people will come on the Day of Resurrection with bright faces, hands, and feet from the traces of *wuḍū'*."[167]

Although it can feel very refreshing to perform the *wuḍū'* during times of hot weather, some people struggle when it is cold or otherwise inconvenient. This is why it holds great reward, because "no one maintains his ablution except a believer."[168] A believer also knows the great feeling of contentment that comes with successfully completing the *wuḍū'* in difficult circumstances.

Note that perfecting the *wuḍū'* does not mean spending excessive amounts of time on it or exaggerating the manner of washing as some mistakenly do.

166. *Riyāḍ al-Ṣāliḥīn* (No. 1059).
167. *Ṣaḥīḥ Muslim* (No. 246).
168. *Sunan Ibn Mājah* (No. 277).

Instead, one can perfect the *wuḍū'* by understanding and adhering to the steps outlined in the Qur'ān.[169]

Some benefits associated with the Islamic practice of *wuḍū'* include the following:

- It washes away one's sins;[170]
- It removes stress, negative thoughts, and evil suggestions from Satan;[171]
- It puts one into a state of cleanliness and purification;[172]
- It provides energy and removes laziness.[173]

Allāh ﷻ also tells us: "**Allāh does not intend to make difficulty for you, but He intends to purify you and complete His favor upon you that you may be grateful.**"[174]

Indeed, this is the case with all obligatory acts of worship, as they are all for our own benefit in the end.

It is reported that Prophet Muḥammad ﷺ once asked his beloved Companion Bilāl ibn Rabāḥ (RA) to describe what deed he had performed after his acceptance of Islām that gave him the most hope of entering Jannah, as the Prophet ﷺ had heard the sound of Bilāl's footsteps in Jannah during a dream, and it is known that the dreams of prophets are, in fact, truthful visions from Allāh ﷻ.

In response, Bilāl (RA) said that the deed that gave him the most hope of entering Jannah was to immediately follow any ablutions he made at any hour of the day or night with prayers (praying for as long as he could).[175]

This demonstrates the importance of *wuḍū'* and prayer, and also shows us that any extra acts of worship we do purely for the sake of Allāh ﷻ make a difference to our status in the Hereafter.

---

169. See Qur'ān 5:6.
170. See *Riyāḍ al-Ṣāliḥīn* (No. 1026).
171. See *Riyāḍ al-Ṣāliḥīn* (No. 1165).
172. See Qur'ān 5:6.
173. See *Riyāḍ al-Ṣāliḥīn* (No. 1165).
174. Qur'ān 5:6.
175. *See Riyāḍ al-Ṣāliḥīn* (No. 1146).

The Prophet ﷺ has also informed us that all the gates of Paradise will be opened for whomever says the following words after completing his *wuḍū'* (so that he may enter through any gate he wishes): "I testify that there is no deity but Allāh alone with no partners, and that Muḥammad is His slave and Messenger."[176]

176. See *Bulūgh al-Marām* (No. 57).

They defeat their anger

"Do not get angry, and Paradise is yours."

— A Saying of Prophet Muḥammad ﷺ (*al-Mu'jam al-Awsaṭ*, No. 2411)

This was the advice of Prophet Muḥammad ﷺ when a Companion of his named Abū al-Dardā' (RA) asked him to tell him about a deed that would admit him to Paradise.

Understand that unrestrained anger provides an easy pathway for Satan to exert his evil influence over the believers.

Once another Companion of the Prophet ﷺ named Sulaymān ibn Ṣurad (RA) was sitting with the Prophet ﷺ when two men began to quarrel and curse each other. One of the men had a visibly red face, and the veins of his neck bulged with rage.

The Prophet ﷺ said (regarding the man): "I know of some words that would dissipate his rage if he were to utter them: 'I seek refuge with Allāh from Satan, the accursed.'"

So, the Companions gathered there told the man: "The Prophet ﷺ tells you to utter: 'I seek refuge with Allāh from Satan, the accursed.'"[177]

This shows us the importance of taking the initiative to help others calm down when we are in the presence of such problems, unlike those who may enjoy inflaming the situation.

But what is so special about restraining one's anger that it helps the believers attain Paradise?

For one, all of the good qualities exhibited by the inhabitants of Jannah in the worldly life of this *dunyā*, such as faith, *taqwá*, patience, reliance on Allāh ﷻ,

177. *Riyāḍ al-Ṣāliḥīn* (No. 46).

maintaining good manners in our speech, and other praiseworthy traits that have been mentioned in this book, can be destroyed in an instant when someone does not work to restrain his anger—and this is because anger can lead to regretful language, losing patience, forgetfulness of Allāh ﷻ, and many other problems.

Of course, we all experience anger at some point in our lives, but those who are wise and successful are conscious of the consequences and make the effort to apply anger management strategies that help avoid the great dangers that come with unrestrained anger—and this effort ultimately results in attaining the pleasure of Allāh ﷻ as well.

Allāh ﷻ mentions this in several verses of the Qur'ān, such as the following:

- "...**And when they are angry, they forgive.**" (Qur'ān 42:37)

  Allāh ﷻ is telling us here about those who will be rewarded by what is "with" Him (Jannah), which is "better and more lasting"[178] than any worldly enjoyment.

- "**Indeed, those who fear Allāh - when an impulse touches them from Satan, they remember [Him] and at once they have insight.**" (Qur'ān 7:201)

  Such people are deserving of Paradise because they are able to remember Allāh ﷻ and act kindly despite any anger they feel.

- "...**And who restrain anger and who pardon the people - and Allāh loves the doers of good.**" (Qur'ān 3:134)

  Here, Allāh ﷻ tells us that the reward of people who restrain their anger is "forgiveness from their Lord and gardens beneath which rivers flow [in Paradise], wherein they will abide eternally."[179]

178. Qur'ān 42:36.
179. Qur'ān 3:136.

With respect to the last verse in particular, we find people who restrain their anger and exhibit other good qualities described by Allāh ﷻ as "al-muḥsinīn" ("the doers of good"), which is derived from the Arabic word "iḥsān," the meaning of which is to perform one's duties in the best possible way, with the intention of excellence and perfection. A person with *iḥsān* feels the presence of Allāh ﷻ and knows that He is watching him and thus behaves accordingly although he cannot physically see Him, also worshiping Allāh in a state of complete mindfulness and devotion.[180]

In order for us to be counted among the doers of good who overcome their anger, we must be willing to work on ourselves and our relationships with Allāh ﷻ.

This is why Allāh ﷻ tells us: "And excellent is the reward of the [righteous] workers."[181] If the way we behave depends solely on how we feel in the heat of the moment, then we have done nothing to contain the emotions that provoke our anger—and the possible fact that one is "short-tempered" can never be an excuse for someone who truly fears Allāh ﷻ.

Below are some practical steps that one can take in order to behave in a manner that is pleasing to Allāh ﷻ during moments of anger:

- **Remain silent.** This was the advice of our beloved Prophet ﷺ when he said: "When you are angry, be silent," repeating the words twice[182] for emphasis. The Prophet ﷺ also said: "Let he who believes in Allāh ﷻ and the Last Day speak good or remain silent."[183]
- **Calm down.** While some people may feel the urge to get up and start a physical fight when angry, the Prophet ﷺ has told us: "If one of you is angry while he is standing, let him sit down so that his anger will leave him; otherwise, let him lie down."[184]

---

180. See *Ṣaḥīḥ al-Bukhārī* (No. 50).
181. Qur'ān 3:136.
182. See *al-Adab al-Mufrad* (No. 1320).
183. See *Riyāḍ al-Ṣāliḥīn* (No. 308).
184. *Sunan Abī Dā'ūd* (No. 4782).

- **Splash your face with cold water.** In addition to the above, perform ablutions (*wuḍū'*), pray, and supplicate to Allāh ﷻ in order to distance yourself from the situation. As Allāh ﷻ tells us: "And seek help through patience and prayer; and indeed, it is difficult except for the humbly submissive [to Allāh ﷻ]."[185]
- **Remember that acting in anger reflects ugliness and weakness.** "A strong person is not someone who physically overpowers others. A strong person is someone who controls himself when angry."[186]
- **Keep your relationship strong with Allāh ﷻ by acting upon this verse from *Sūrat al-A'rāf*:**

  "And remember your Lord within yourself in humility and in fear without being apparent in speech - in the mornings and the evenings. And do not be among the heedless."[188]
- **If it happened that you unintentionally wronged someone through your anger, take steps to repent and fix the situation.**
- **Always remind yourself of the great rewards associated with restraining anger.** "Whoever swallows his anger, then Allāh will conceal his faults. Whoever suppresses his rage, even though he could fulfill his anger if he wished, then Allāh will secure his heart on the Day of Resurrection."[189]

185. Qur'ān 2:45.
186. *al-Adab al-Mufrad* (No. 1317).
187. Because keeping your remembrance of Allāh ﷻ private (between you and Allāh ﷻ) is closer to honesty and sincerity.
188. Qur'ān 7:205.
189. A saying of Prophet Muḥammad ﷺ (*al-Mu'jam al-Awsaṭ*, No. 6026).

They are soft-hearted

"It [Hell-Fire] is forbidden upon every person who is warm (friendly), lenient, tender, and easy to get along with."

— A Saying of Prophet Muḥammad ﷺ (*Riyāḍ al-Ṣāliḥīn*, No. 641)

This *ḥadīth* tells us that the way one deals with people could be his or her free pass to Jannah.

In order to fit the description of the *ḥadīth*, one should strive to be:

- Empathetic;
- Considerate;
- Open-minded and soft-hearted;
- Easy to talk to and deal with;
- Polite, even when expressing disagreement or criticism.

Such people typically:

- Make matters easy for people when in a position to do so;
- Apologize easily and accept other people's apologies without a fuss;
- Tend to be calm and composed and do not intentionally hurt or annoy others;
- Choose the easiest path when presented with two or more choices.

People who are easy-going and pleasant to be around have usually first cultivated a strong sense of inner-peace and contentment within their own selves.

The opposite of these praiseworthy qualities is found in people who display stubbornness, selfishness, and hardness of the heart—and while people often naturally vary in their temperaments since the very beginning stages of childhood, there are certain things a person can do to rid him or herself of these negative personality traits (if present) in order to become more merciful and easy-going by Allāh's will.

When a man once complained to Prophet Muḥammad ﷺ about having a hard heart, the Prophet ﷺ advised him to feed the poor and be kind to an orphan.[190]

Other than performing various types of voluntary community service, which helps us feel with others and become more understanding of different life circumstances, one can also soften the heart by:

- **Reflecting upon the Qur'ān.** Allāh ﷻ tells us that if the Qur'ān had been sent upon something as hard as a mountain, "you would have seen it humbled and splitting from fear of Allāh."[191] So how about a human's heart? Would it not soften?
- **Remembering death and visiting graves.** The act of contemplating death helps one remember that the worldly life of this *dunyā* is not as important as one may think, as death will eventually overtake each and every one of us. As such, we should be prepared for our Hereafter and deal kindly with others while we still have the chance. Prophet Muḥammad ﷺ said: "Be merciful on the earth, and you will be shown mercy from He Who is above the heavens."[192]
- **Reading the biography of Prophet Muḥammad ﷺ.** The stories found in the Prophet's biography provide profound examples of his extraordinary kindness and softness of the heart in many different circumstances, showing us how the Prophet ﷺ behaved in his roles as a family man, a teacher, and the leader of a nation.

190. See *Musnad Aḥmad* (2/263).
191. Qur'ān 59:21.
192. *Jāmi' al-Tirmidhī* (No. 1924).

Among these stories is that a Bedouin man once came to the mosque while the Prophet ﷺ and his Companions were there and urinated on the ground without any regard for the sanctity of the place. The Muslims were upset by what they saw and got up to scold the man, but the Prophet ﷺ told them not to interrupt him. After that, he told the Companions to clean that spot with water and gently took the Bedouin aside and told him that mosques are not places meant for urine and filth, but are rather "only for the remembrance of Allāh, prayer, and the recitation of the Qur'ān."[193]

A similar story took place when a Companion who was still new to Islām did not know that it was inappropriate to speak during prayer and said "May Allāh have mercy upon you" out loud when another man sneezed while they were praying one day alongside the Prophet ﷺ. Some other Companions who were also praying were disturbed by this and showed displeasure by striking their hands against their thighs. The Prophet ﷺ himself, however, continued praying and did not rebuke the man after he finished, but instead kindly explained to him that one should not speak to others during prayer, as the prayer is solely for the purpose of glorifying Allāh ﷻ and reciting the Qur'ān.

The man then said that he had never seen a better teacher than the Prophet ﷺ.[194] If only those teachers who continuously put their students down could learn from the prophetic approach that shows us in the most beautiful of ways how to have a positive influence on others.

It is worth mentioning that Allāh ﷻ draws attention to the qualities of mercy and compassion in different verses of the Qur'ān, such as when He describes the believers as "**merciful among themselves**"[195] and says that "**their sign is in their faces from the effect of prostration [i.e., prayer],**"[196] which shows that someone who prays with the intention of pleasing the Creator already possesses such qualities. These are the people whom Allāh ﷻ promises Jannah.[197]

193. See *Ṣaḥīḥ Muslim* (No. 285).
194. See *Ṣaḥīḥ Muslim* (No. 537).
195. Qur'ān 48:29.
196. Qur'ān 48:29.
197. Qur'ān 48:29.

Allāh ﷻ also describes the believers as those who "**advised one another to patience and advised one another to compassion**" and says that "**those are the companions of the right.**"[198] The "companions of the right" are those who will receive their record of deeds on the Day of Judgment in their right hands, which is a sign that they are about to enter Jannah.

197. Qur'ān 48:29.
198. Qur'ān 90:17–18.

THEY FOLLOW THE PATH OF ALLĀH ﷻ

"We will call forth every people with their *imām* [leader]."

— *Sūrat al-Isrā'* (Qur'ān 17:71)

Who is your greatest role model in life, and where do you take most of your influences from?

These are important questions that we should all take the time to contemplate on a deeper level.

Could you, yourself, be a role model for other people to follow? And what kind of influence do you have on others?

These, too, are important questions that deserve careful thought.

With so many different entities out there who can easily provide unlimited content nowadays to a large number of followers for mass consumption, it is important every now and then to re-evaluate the ideas we have (sometimes unconsciously) started to adopt and believe in so that we make sure whether these new ideas are actually compatible with the teachings of Islām.

In the verse from *Sūrat al-Isrā'* quoted at the start of this passage (Qur'ān 17:71), Allāh ﷻ tells us that all people will be summoned before Him on the Day of Judgment along with the specific *imām* (leader) they followed in this *dunyā*. Each person will then receive his or her personalized record of deeds showing everything that took place during that person's journey to the Hereafter.

While different interpretations of this verse exist, some scholars have said that the referenced "leader" may be a person, a book of scripture, or a school of thought.[199]

199. Other explanations state that the "imām" mentioned in this verse instead refers to one's record of deeds.

As mentioned earlier, a reassuring sign for those destined for Jannah is that they will receive their records in their right hands, which will indicate that they followed the appropriate leader. For believing Muslims who are among the *ummah* (nation) of Prophet Muḥammad ﷺ, this will have meant following the Prophet ﷺ as well as the Glorious Qur'ān.

As Allāh ﷻ informs us in the Qur'ān, those who receive their records in their right hands will be so overjoyed that they will share the good news by asking others to read what their records contain;[200] they will also have an "easy reckoning"[201] before going on to live a "life of Bliss in an elevated garden (Jannah)."[202]

In contrast, those who are blind in this life, refusing to see the truth that would take them on the path to Jannah, will also remain astray in the Hereafter.[203] After receiving their records of deeds in their left hands,[204] they will be so ashamed of what these records contain that they will hide them behind their backs,[205] wishing they had never been given their records or known anything of their reckoning in the Hereafter. Instead, they will wish that their lives had permanently ended with death rather than continuing into eternity.[206]

Based on what we know of such people in the Qur'ān, one can deduce that they did not take steps to protect their souls from destructive inclinations in the worldly life of this *dunyā* and ended up following "leaders" in transgression and corruption, giving them undue status as role models and influencers.

On their path to Hell-Fire, the corrupt leaders and their followers will be stopped and questioned.[207] "[They will be asked], 'What is [wrong] with you? Why do you not help each other?'"[208]

200. Qur'ān 69:19.
201. Qur'ān 84:8.
202. Qur'ān 69:21–22.
203. Qur'ān 17:72.
204. Qur'ān 69:25.
205. Qur'ān 84:10.
206. See Qur'ān 69:25–27.
207. See Qur'ān 37:23–24.
208. Qur'ān 37:25.

Instead of helping each other, however (which they will be powerless to do in the first place), they will start to blame each other, with the followers telling their leaders that they prevented them from goodness with the power and influence they had over them, and the corrupt leaders saying in response: "Rather, you [yourselves] were not believers. And we had over you no authority, but you were a transgressing people."[209]

This is why the fate of both groups is ultimately the same, as Allāh ﷻ tells us: "So indeed they, that Day, will be sharing in the punishment."[210]

In the end, let this be a reminder that no soul can be excused for choosing the wrong path, whether that person is a leader or a mere follower, as Allāh ﷻ has already "inspired it [the soul] [with discernment of] its wickedness and its righteousness."[211]

The secret to staying on the path of truth and goodness is to work on purifying the soul in order to attain the traits of a believer that Allāh ﷻ describes in the Qur'ān. Whenever the opposite happens, know that there is something wrong with your choices.

"But as for he who feared the position of his Lord and prevented the soul from [unlawful] inclination, then indeed, Paradise will be [his] refuge."[212]

---

209. See Qur'ān 37:26–30.

210. Qur'ān 37:33.

211. Qur'ān 91:8.

212. Qur'ān 79:40–41.

THEY VISIT THE SICK

"He who visits the sick is harvesting the fruits of Paradise until he returns."

— A Saying of Prophet Muḥammad ﷺ (*Ṣaḥīḥ Muslim*, No. 2568)

Visiting the sick is a means for one to be granted great bounties in Jannah, as it is a caring act that serves to comfort and console others, which is among the most beloved deeds to Allāh ﷻ. This is confirmed by the words of Prophet Muḥammad ﷺ, who said: "**The most beloved of deeds to Allāh, may He be exalted, is bringing joy to a Muslim.**"[213]

The Prophet ﷺ was the best example of implementing this good deed and advising the Muslims to make it a regular habit as well, as witnessed by his Companions (may Allāh ﷻ be pleased with them all). 'Uthmān ibn 'Affān (RA), for example, narrated that he accompanied the Prophet ﷺ to many different places. Even while traveling, he witnessed the Prophet ﷺ visiting the sick, attending people's funerals, and comforting people with whatever means he could.[214]

But in order for our visits to be conducted in a way that is pleasing to Allāh ﷻ, there are certain common-sense etiquettes that should be observed when visiting the sick, some of which are listed below:

- Choosing times that are convenient for the patient and do not cause him disturbance or embarrassment;
- Keeping visits relatively short so that the patient is not burdened by your presence;
- Maintaining positive energy during the visit (perhaps even incorporating humor when possible) so that the visit is one that brings comfort to the patient rather than feelings of depression or sadness;

213. *al-Targhīb wa-al-Tarhīb* (No. 2623).
214. *Musnad Aḥmad* (No. 504).

- Maintaining a calm and pleasant tone so that the patient does not feel annoyed by the sound of your voice;
- Remaining quiet if it is apparent that the patient wishes to sleep or relax.

It is also recommended in Islām to make special supplications for the sick. As reported by the Prophet's wife 'Ā'ishah (RA): "When Allāh's Messenger ﷺ came to visit anyone sick, he supplicated for him and said: '**Lord of the people, remove the malady and cure him (the sick person), for You are The Great Curer. There is no cure but through Your healing Power that leaves no trace of illness.**'"[215]

While the priority should be given to the people we know, it is also praiseworthy to visit strangers (whether in hospitals or elsewhere) with the intention of bringing happiness to the hearts of those who are ill.

One should not underestimate the great reward associated with this simple act of goodness. As narrated by Prophet Muḥammad ﷺ in a *ḥadīth qudsī*, Allāh ﷻ will tell those who did not make effort to visit the sick on the Day of Judgment: "O Son of Ādam, I was ill and you did not visit Me." The person will say: "O Lord, how could I visit You when You are the Lord of the universe?" Allāh ﷻ will tell him: "Did you not know that My servant so-and-so was ill? If you had visited him, you would have found that deed with Me [as a reward]."[216]

215. *Ṣaḥīḥ Muslim* (No. 2191d).
216. See *al-Adab Al-Mufrad* (No. 517). Another translation says: "You would have found Me with him."

They are doers of good

"For them who have done good is the best [reward] - and extra."

— *Sūrat Yūnus* (Qur'ān 10:26)

The best reward is Jannah, of course.

But what is meant by "extra"?

In relation to this verse of the Qur'ān, Prophet Muḥammad ﷺ said that when those deserving of Paradise enter Jannah, Allāh ﷻ will say to them: "Do you wish for Me to give you anything extra?" They will say: "Did You not brighten our faces? Did You not admit us into Paradise and save us from Hell-Fire?"[217]

This is when the Mantle will be lifted [from The Most Merciful's Face]—and with all of the bounties given to the people of Jannah, there will be nothing dearer to them than looking at their Lord.[218] They are described in the Qur'ān as having "radiant faces" due to how much pleasure they will have gained.[219]

Most of us have undoubtedly experienced feelings of serenity, peace, and joy in the worldly life of this *dunyā* when surrounded by the beauty of Allāh's creation (such as when we take a walk in the forest or see a pretty sunset)—so just imagine the dazzling beauty of the Creator Himself! Yet Allāh's perfect beauty is something that does not belong to the life of this world; it is a special kind of beauty that remains known only to Him, yet reading about the names and attributes of Allāh ﷻ can provide us with insights as to what this vast and indescribable beauty encompasses.

As for those destined for the fires of Hell, they will be "partitioned" and deprived of the ability to see Allāh ﷻ.[220]

---

217. Meaning: "What more could anyone wish for?"

218. See *Ṣaḥīḥ Muslim* (No. 181a).

219. See Qur'ān 75:22–23, 83:24.

220. See Qur'ān 83:15.

As a result, their faces will be dark with humiliation due to all of the evil they committed in this *dunyā* instead of choosing the path of goodness when they still had the chance.[221]

According to the verse quoted at the start of this passage (Qur'ān 10:26), the people who will have the privilege of seeing Allāh ﷻ in the Hereafter are those who have done good in this *dunyā*.

Since the description here is broad, the meaning is also broad.

These people will have done good in their acts of worship (with the intention of pleasing Allāh ﷻ).

They will have done good in other aspects of their lives as well, never hesitating to choose the path of goodness when dealing with others and performing good deeds of benefit to their families, their communities, the world at large, and even themselves.

This is a message for all of us: **Do not hesitate to perform good deeds**, no matter how simple or uncommon your idea is.

Sometimes we may underestimate the idea for a good deed that has occurred to us, but Allāh ﷻ tells us that "**whoever does an atom's weight of good [in this *dunyā*] will see it [i.e., its effect in the Hereafter].**"[222]

Your positive, uplifting words... your smiles... the assistance you provide to others... your attempts to reconcile between people... even the kindness you show to animals... **they all count.**

Another simple good deed that one should not neglect is that of repelling evil with goodness. For example, if someone is avoiding you and does not greet you when you cross paths, initiate the greeting of *salām* (peace) between you! Taking the initiative in such circumstances has the effect of setting a good example for others and also helps spread goodness in society, hence the great reward associated with such acts.

221. See Qur'ān 10:27.
222. Qur'ān 99:7.

Of course, it may feel difficult at times to initiate goodness with people who do not seem to appreciate your efforts, but we can always try to maintain a healthy attitude and mindset when dealing with such people by renewing our intentions, as this helps us remember that one's good deeds should only be for the sake of Allāh ﷻ, and not for the sake of receiving gratitude or special favors from anyone in return. At the same time, if people do, in fact, show gratitude in certain situations and reform for the better, then all praise and gratitude is due to Allāh ﷻ.

Adopting this way of thinking helps one cultivate the quality of patience in order to maintain the goodness in one's own heart when dealing with difficult people.

"O Allāh, I ask You for the delight of gazing upon Your Face and the joy of meeting You [in the Hereafter]!"[223]

223. A supplication from *Ḥiṣn al-Muslim* (No. 62).

They are just

"The just will be seated upon pulpits of light."

— A Saying of Prophet Muḥammad ﷺ (*Ṣaḥīḥ Muslim*, No. 1827)

This *ḥadīth* goes on to tell us that people who are just in the worldly life of this *dunyā* will be among those closest to Allāh ﷻ in Jannah, as they will be elevated in position and seated to Allāh's right!

But what does it mean to be just?

While the characteristic of being just is commonly associated with leaders, judges, and people in high positions who handle people's affairs, it is actually the duty of each and every one of us to be just on this earth wherever justice is required, which may be in matters pertaining to our work, our families, our communities, and even our own selves.

Among the rights you should not deprive yourself of are:

- Living a healthy lifestyle, which includes diet, exercise, and the quality of your sleep, in addition to routine medical check-ups;
- Maintaining a healthy spiritual relationship with Allāh ﷻ by adherence to prayer, reading the Qur'ān, and basic Islamic principles, all of which protect one from fear, emptiness, and temptation;
- Refraining from prohibited acts that lead one astray and damage the soul;
- Setting respectful boundaries when needed and striving for healthy relationships by cultivating an Islamic character that is pleasing to Allāh ﷻ;
- Continuously educating oneself through reading and building new life experiences.

As for protecting the rights of others, everyone we know or encounter has the right to good treatment, whether they are family members, relatives, neighbors, friends, people at work, or even passing acquaintances. How justice is applied will vary according to one's specific role in a particular relationship; for example, it is a parent's responsibility to be fair with all of his or her children and not show undue favoritism to one over the other.

Justice also requires one to be truthful when offering testimony.

The overall concept of justice in Islām is outlined in these two verses of the Qur'ān:

- "O you who have believed, be persistently standing firm for Allāh, witnesses in justice, and do not let the hatred of a people prevent you from being just. Be just; that is nearer to righteousness. And fear Allāh; indeed, Allāh is [fully] Aware of what you do." (Qur'ān 5:8)
- "O you who have believed, be persistently standing firm in justice, witnesses for Allāh, even if it be against yourselves or parents and relatives. Whether one is rich or poor, Allāh is more worthy of both. So follow not [personal] inclination, lest you not be just. And if you distort [your testimony] or refuse [to give it], then indeed Allāh is ever, of what you do, Aware." (Qur'ān 4:135)

A Muslim should beware of causing injustice to anyone. Prophet Muḥammad ﷺ once asked his Companions: "Do you know who is the bankrupt?" They said: "The bankrupt among us is he who has neither money nor any property." The Prophet ﷺ said: "The bankrupt of my *ummah* (nation) will be those who come on the Day of Resurrection [accompanied by the good deeds of] prayer, fasting, and charity [but will find themselves bankrupt on that day] because **they reviled others, slandered them, unlawfully devoured their wealth, shed their blood, and beat them**, so their good deeds will be credited to the accounts of those [who suffered due to these injustices]. If such a person's good deeds fall short to clear the account, his sins will be entered into his account until he is thrown into Hell-Fire [because no good deeds will be left for him]."[224]

We should all examine our current and past deeds to assess whether we have ever caused injustice to anyone in this life so that we can make amends while we still have the chance by Allāh's will.

"Indeed, Allāh loves those who act justly."[225]

It is also worth mentioning that our Ever-Merciful Lord Who loves for people to implement justice in this *dunyā* will also use the approach of justice with each and every one of us on the Day of Judgment, yet His justice is completely free of shortcomings.

"So today [i.e., the Day of Judgement] no soul will be wronged at all, and you will not be recompensed except for what you used to do. Indeed, the companions of Paradise, that Day, will be amused in [joyful] occupation - they and their kinds - in shade, reclining on adorned couches. For them therein is fruit, and for them is whatever they request [or wish]. And 'Peace!' will be [their] greeting from the Merciful Lord."[226]

224. See *Riyāḍ al-Ṣāliḥīn* (No. 218).
225. Qur'ān 49:9.
226. Qur'ān 36:54–58.

THEY GATHER WITH OTHERS TO SPREAD RIGHTEOUSNESS

"We [angels] were your allies in worldly life and [are so] in the Hereafter."

— *Sūrat Fuṣṣilat* (Qur'ān 41:31)

While it's a given that the All-Knowing Allāh ﷻ is not in need of any helpers to record our deeds or tell Him about us, it is because of His great justice and mercy upon us that He has appointed angels to perform certain tasks and duties on His behalf, and this includes creating a record of our deeds that we are presented with on the Day of Judgment.

This detailed and precise record allows us to review all of the evidence for and against us so that there can be no doubt as to the final verdict and whether it is one that is just.

Contrast this with a courtroom devoid of witnesses or lawyers, where it is only the judge and the judged, without the benefit of expert testimony or the ability to understand the charges against you.

A key feature of Allāh's supreme system of justice in the Hereafter is that the angels will be truthful witnesses to the deeds we have done in the worldly life of this *dunyā*. In addition, they will also take on the role of being devoted friends to the believers, serving as extra support for them.

How is that?

See the below passage from *Sūrat Ghāfir*:

"Those [angels] who carry the Throne and those around it exalt [Allāh ﷻ] with praise of their Lord and believe in Him and ask forgiveness for those who have believed, [saying], '**Our Lord, You have encompassed all things in mercy and knowledge, so forgive those who have repented and followed Your way**

and protect them from the punishment of Hell-Fire. Our Lord, and admit them to gardens of perpetual residence which You have promised them and whoever was righteous among their forefathers, their spouses, and their offspring. Indeed, it is You who is the Exalted in Might, the Wise. And protect them from the evil consequences [of their deeds]. And he whom You protect from evil consequences that Day - You will have given him mercy. And that is the great attainment.'"[227]

These verses show us that the angels will act as witnesses for the believers each time they do a good deed in this *dunyā* and will also be their mediators in the Hereafter. They will make a special request to Allāh ﷻ to forgive and reward those who did not insist upon their sins—and they will also ask Allāh ﷻ out of mercy and concern for these people's happiness that they be reunited with their believing family members in Jannah.

This is unlike those who have taken the path of evil in this *dunyā*; among the punishments such people will endure is that they will not be defended by the angels in the Hereafter, and they will also experience the disappointment of being let down by those who were their evil allies in this worldly life. In a state of regret, the disbelievers will then say: "By Allāh, we were indeed in manifest error"[228] ... "so now we have no intercessors, and not a devoted friend. If only we could return [to the world] and be of the believers...."[229]

Other than what we know from the Qur'ān about the people whom the angels will support (that they are humble, repenting believers), several sayings of Prophet Muḥammad ﷺ inform us that **gathering with people for the purpose of remembering Allāh ﷻ or learning about Islām and the Qur'ān** is a means for one to be surrounded by the angels, who will later praise those who attended such gatherings when telling Allāh ﷻ about them.

As a result, <u>everyone</u> who attended such gatherings will be rewarded, even if some present happen to be less righteous than others who are there.

227. Qur'ān 40:7–9.
228. Qur'ān 26:97.
229. Qur'ān 26:100–102.

Their reward will be that "tranquility will descend upon them, mercy will engulf them," and Allāh ﷻ will also grant them His pardon. One of the angels will say: "Our Lord, there is amongst them such-and-such person [who does not belong to the assembly of those who are participating in Your remembrance]. He [only] passed by and sat down with them." Then Allāh ﷻ will say: "I also grant him pardon because they are the people by virtue of whom their associates will not be unfortunate."[230]

Keeping the above in mind, let us all take advantage of our short time on Earth, doing whatever we can to gain the great privilege of friendship with the angels. We should also not forget that those of us alive today are blessed with certain conveniences that did not exist in the past, such as the ability to organize online gatherings with friends and other believers from around the world for the purpose of learning more about Islām.

The angels record all of our deeds until our time in this *dunyā* has come to an end, so let us always aim for the best of deeds!

"And He (Allāh ﷻ) sends over you guardian-angels until, when death comes to one of you, Our messengers [i.e., angels of death] take him, and they do not fail [in their duties]."[231]

230. For reference, see *Riyāḍ al-Ṣāliḥīn* (Nos. 1023 and 1447).

231. Qur'ān 6:61.

∘ Author's Note & Conclusion ∘

"The ones whom the angels take in death, [being] good and pure; [the angels] will say, 'Peace be upon you. Enter Paradise for what you used to do.'"

— *Sūrat al-Naḥl* (Qur'ān 16:32)

In order for us to cross over the threshold that separates us from the permanent abode of the Hereafter, we must first experience the finality of death in this temporary world of trials and tests.

The duration of these tests is unique to each individual and known only to Allāh ﷻ alone. What is certain, however, is that there is no turning back when one's time finally comes.

While people are generally naturally very uncomfortable with the prospect of unfamiliar experiences that contain elements of fear and uncertainty, Allāh ﷻ comforts His believers regarding this issue, telling them that their experience with death and entering the world of the unseen will be a positive one.

Again, we find that the angels will be present with them as protective friends to comfort them at the time of death; they will greet them and convey glad tidings to them, saying: "**Do not fear and do not grieve, but receive good tidings of Paradise, which you were promised. We [angels] were your allies in worldly life and [are so] in the Hereafter. And you will have therein whatever your souls desire, and you will have therein whatever you request [or wish] as accommodation from a [Lord who is] Forgiving and Merciful.**"[232]

One can only imagine the immense peace and comfort that a believer will feel upon hearing these words despite the fact that he or she is in the midst of departing from all that is dear and familiar in the worldly life of this *dunyā*.

If you have ever mourned the loss of a loved one, use this information to transform all of the sadness you have ever felt over this person's death into

232. See Qur'ān 41:30–32.

prayers and supplications for him or her to be among the privileged inhabitants of Jannah.

We, too, must strive hard to be among these privileged inhabitants so that we are ready when the time comes to meet Allāh ﷻ with our deeds from this life, keeping in mind that: **"When a man dies, his deeds come to an end except for three: ongoing charity; knowledge that is beneficial; or a virtuous descendant who prays for him."**[233]

With that, my dear readers, I end this book with the hope that Allāh ﷻ accepts my work as a good deed that has a positive influence on others. *Āmīn.*

Let us take it as a mission upon ourselves to start changing for the better and making the most out of our time left in this *dunyā*.

I hope you have enjoyed and benefited from all of the valuable information this book contains from the Qur'ān and *sunnah* about Jannah and the path we should take in order to reach it—and know that so long as you strive to do good in this life, Allāh ﷻ will reward you with good and what is even much better, *in shā' Allāh.*

May we all be guided to be among the people whom Allāh ﷻ is pleased with and promises Jannah. *Āmīn.*

Finally, please don't forget me and my family in your sincere supplications.

"The supplication of a Muslim for his (Muslim) brother in his absence will certainly be answered. Every time he makes a supplication for good for his brother, the angel appointed for this particular task says: '*Āmīn*! May it be for you, too.'"[234]

Your sister in Islām,

Naima Abdullah

233. A saying of Prophet Muḥammad ﷺ (*Riyāḍ al-Ṣāliḥīn*, No. 1383).
234. *Riyāḍ al-Ṣāliḥīn* (No. 1495).

Printed in Great Britain
by Amazon

33737607R00061